THE RISE AND FALL
OF THE SOVIET THREAT:
Domestic Sources
of the Cold War Consensus

Library of Congress Catalog Card Number: 83-051285
ISBN: 0-89608-206-7 (paper)
ISBN: 0-89608-207-5 (cloth)

Cover design by Ann Raszmann

SOUTH END PRESS
302 COLUMBUS AVENUE
BOSTON, MA 02116

To Rebekka

ACKNOWLEDGEMENTS

This project originated at the urging of the Institute for Policy Studies, where Steve Daggett and Michael Klare were enormously helpful. Indeed, without Michael's patience and persistence, neither that version nor the present rewriting would ever have occurred. The editorial collective of South End Press provided numerous suggestions which helped improve the argument. Finally, Jytte Klausen insisted time after time that I bring this analysis up to date and get it into print. She knows how much I appreciate it.

Alan Wolfe
Brooklyn, New York
Labor Day, 1983

TABLE OF CONTENTS

CHAPTER I

THE DOMESTIC BASIS
OF THE SOVIET THREAT

The Soviet Union has used detente to build the biggest
military force the world has ever seen…The Soviet navy now
has a blue-ocean navy for the first time in their history and it's
far more than a two-ocean navy. It is aimed at intercepting the
some sixteen choke points in the world…We are losing
through obsolescence and accident more airplanes each year
than we're building. Our Air Force is getting—our air might is
getting smaller…The Soviet Union has used its own military
instead of proxy troops, and this bespeaks an arrogance and a
confidence born of their military strength, that they made
that move, and we have been sending the wrong signals.
We've been sending the kind of signals that made that
possible, and what we need to do is send them some signals
that let them know that there is a point beyond which they
cannot go in the world without risking a direct confrontation
with us.

Ronald Reagan, quoted by Robert Scheer
during the 1980 campaign.

"Let's not delude ourselves," Ronald Reagan said in 1981.
"The Soviet Union underlies all the unrest that is going on. If they
weren't engaged in this game of dominoes, there wouldn't be any

hot spots in the world."[1] Not since the cold war began, and perhaps never before in American history, has an administration come to power with as insistently hostile an attitude toward the Soviet Union as that of Ronald Reagan.

The new president, however, was not alone in his views about the Russians. A dual perception that the Russians were getting stronger while America was becoming weaker grew in strength during the late 1970s. Spurred by a whole host of conservative and neo-conservative organizations like the Committee on the Present Danger, an aura of fear about Soviet intentions first led the Carter Administration to reverse course and then contributed to the atmosphere in which the election of Reagan became possible. Once in office, the Reagan Administration practiced what it preached, bringing the Committee on the Present Danger into the halls of power. In a study of 100 top officials in the Reagan Administration, researchers discovered that 32 of them, including Secretary of State George P. Schultz, were members of the Committee.[2] CPD stalwarts like Eugene Rostow and Paul Nitze were placed in charge of negotiating with the Russians, yet so charged was the atmosphere that these life-long superhawks were viewed by the press, and perhaps by themselves, as moderates; Rostow was even fired by the Administration. Reagan s election brought to its logical conclusion the feeling that a preoccupation with Soviet power should be placed at the core of American foreign policy.

The Reagan Administration lost little time trying to translate its perception of an overarching Soviet threat into policy. Immediately upon entering office, Mr. Reagan proposed vast increases in military spending—this at a time when, he said, economic austerity demanded cuts in every other area of expenditure. Statements from the White House accused the Soviet leadership of lying and alleged that the Russians were behind nearly all incidents of political instability throughout the world. New weapons, from chemical warfare to strategic systems, were advocated, and the Administration made clear its suspicion of arms control agreements with an antagonist deemed so untrustworthy.

As time went by, the Reagan Administration's relentless quest for military strength, combined with its often confused responses to global crises, led to the charge that no encompassing worldview or political philosophy was guiding the Administration's actions. "The Reagan Administration has been accused," Secretary of Defense Weinberger said at the Council on Foreign Relations in April 1982, "of having no clear defense policy or military strategy." Weinberger went on to assure the assembled guests that this perception was not true. America desired a stable world dominated by "free" nations, but, he continued, these goals could not be obtained in the face of Soviet conduct. "In the post-war period the primary challenge to our successful pursuit of these goals has been from the Soviet Union. For the past 30 years, rapidly growing Soviet conventional and nuclear forces have provided the major threats to our own survival and that of our allies. Soviet global expansion has posed the major obstacle to world peace and stability."[3]

While Weinberger was articulating these thoughts, the Administration was fervishly working on a statement of its principles. Leaked to the press in various forms during May 1982, the resulting memos and position papers indicated that a great deal of attention was given to the Soviet threat. For example, in his first speech after becoming Mr. Reagan's national security advisor, William P. Clark drew on an internal National Security Decision Memorandum to suggest that the goal of the Administration was to "establish priorities for sequential operations to insure that military power would be applied in the most effective ways."[4] Less than two weeks later, Secretary Weinberger told the Army War College in Carlisle Barracks, Pa. that the Administration was committed to the need to be able to fight a prolonged nuclear war against the Soviet Union.[5] This speech in turn was based upon a 126-page internal "guidance document" premised upon the proposition that the U.S. must develop the capacity to survive and win a nuclear war in order to "deter" a possible Soviet attack. By the summer of 1982, in short, the Reagan Administration had gone further than any previous administration in postwar U.S. history in adopting the point of view that the Russians were a direct and imminent threat to the security of the United States. The Administration even published a booklet called *Soviet Military Power* touting the strength and invincibility of its opponent. (The Russians, not to be outdone, published a book of their own on the American military build-up.)

The position of the Reagan Administration was not advanced without provoking considerable controversy, since it was once accepted by most specialists that "winning" is an irrelevant concept in an all-out nuclear exchange. Disagreement with the Reagan Administration's views was unusually sharp; Tom Wicker, who took the lead among newspaper columnists in devoting his energies to this issue, called the planning document of the Administration a "blueprint for turning uneasy Soviet-American relations into an unrelenting war to the death."[6] A national debate, certainly long overdue, began over the question of nuclear war planning, and the American people, convinced as recently as 1980 that their military security was threatened, suddenly began to yearn for a freeze on the further deployment of new nuclear weapons systems. Meanwhile the Russians continued their policy of building new weapons while calling for East-West talks. (All talks between the Soviet Union and the United States were suspended in December 1983 as the first U.S. missiles arrived in Western Europe. Though these talks may resume, relations between the superpowers as 1984 begins are at their worst point since the Cold War began.)

American public opinion is now wildly polarized over issues involving nuclear war planning, with the Reagan Administration, though publicly pledged to talks with the Soviets, clearly anxious to build new weapons, and a growing peace movement just as clearly dedicated to stopping them. Even within the defense community and the foreign policy establishment there is an intense debate over Soviet military power, as former officials of both parties have published manifestos calling for negotiations or for various confidence-building mechanisms. Behind all these positions lie sharp disagreements over the nature of the threat from the Soviet Union. From the Reagan Administration's perspective the Russians are an aggressive and revolutionary power, stoppable only through toughness. To Reagan's critics, the Russians are not especially trusted but the threat to global peace is seen as coming from an arms race in which both superpowers bear some of the blame. An answer to the question of which side is correct can perhaps be found by looking more carefully at the role that negative perceptions of the Soviet threat have played in American political life. In this book I will suggest that past periods of consensus about the immediacy of the Soviet threat have had as much to do with domestic factors inside the United States as with Soviet foreign policy, making inherently suspicious, if not quite dangerous, the Reagan Administration's attempts to prepare to fight a nuclear war in order to prevent one.

The debate that broke out about Russian intentions in the early years of the Reagan Administration was not a new phenomenon. Nor was the influence of an organization like the Committee on the Present Danger. (Indeed, this committee borrowed both its name and its purpose from an organization founded in 1950 to warn the United States about the consequences of the Russian detonation of atomic weapons.) From time to time, one or another group of "hard-line" defense specialists has issued chilling reports about the nature of Soviet intentions. There was in 1945 the so-called "long telegram" written by George Kennan from Moscow, which warned State Department officials about an inherent tendency of Russia to expand. There was NSC-68, a 1950 top-secret review of Soviet intentions, which prophesized a red future unless the U.S. responded quickly. In 1957, the Gaither Report warned that the U.S. was falling behind the Soviets and needed to regain the initiative. Best-selling books in the late 1950s by Maxwell Taylor and Henry Kissinger warned of America's weakness. More recently, a team of intelligence specialists commissioned by President Ford—called "Team B"—spoke menacingly of a major Soviet military build-up. In opposition to President Carter's attempts to win support for the Strategic Arms Limitation Treaty with the Soviet Union, a phalanx of Cold War organizations, of which the Committee on the Present Danger was among the more moderate, sprang into life. Now that a committed conservative is President of the United States, not all these groups are happy; the Heritage Foundation, for one, has found Ronald Reagan insufficiently hawkish for its tastes.

Each time the fear of the Soviet threat has leaped into American consciousness, it has also subsequently subsided. The Cold War of the late 1940s gave way to Eisenhower's (relative) placidity. The missile gap and war scares of the early 1960s were followed by detente. Even Reagan's military plans, warmly supported by the American people in 1980, were viewed more suspiciously within a matter of just two years. By September 1983, the downing by the Soviet Union of an unarmed passenger jet, which two years earlier would have been used by the Reagan Administration to cancel agreements with the Soviet Union, was met more with rhetoric than with suspension of wheat deals and arms control talks. The U.S. perception of the Soviet threat, in a word, rises and falls quite regularly, demanding some explanation of why it is that at some points in time Americans worry about the Russians to the exclusion of just about everything else, while at other points Americans withdraw their attention from the world and put domestic considerations first.

The easiest answer to the ups and downs of American attitudes towards the Russians puts the blame on the Russians. To the more hawkishly inclined, there is no intellectual problem here worth considering. When the Russians become more hostile— invading other countries, increasing their military spending, stepping up their rhetoric—the U.S. has no choice but to respond. If the Russians gave up their expansionist ambitions—and perhaps reformed their internal society as well—then there would be no excessive concern in the United States about the Soviet threat.

Such a point of view is not restricted to the political right. From the left as well, there are some who argue that the reason why the United States becomes more suspicious of the Soviet Union is because the Russians have become more of an obstacle to American global ambitions. The most extreme version of this theory that I have heard occurred when I presented a series of lectures detailing the themes of this book at the Institute for the Study of the United States and Canada in Moscow. I had previously been criticized by conservative audiences for ignoring the "real nature" of the Soviet threat; on this occasion I heard it from the Russians themselves. All your focus on American domestic politics, they told me, is irrelevant; the U.S. is afraid of us because of our unflinching support for revolutionary peoples and movements around the globe. Back home, I have heard versions of this argument in many places, based on Soviet support for liberation struggles in the Third World or on the capacity of the Russians to "catch up" to the United States in military hardware, thereby constricting America's freedom of movement in world affairs.

In this book I will reject the argument that Soviet foreign policy—in either the right-wing or left-wing version—is responsible for the rise and fall of the Soviet threat in American perceptions. I have found that the idea that America has become weaker while the Russians have gained was not true in the past and is not true at present. As far as I can see, the U.S. has been, and remains, the number one military power in the world. True, the Russians have narrowed the gap, but this is a process that has been taking place consistently since 1945, without the sharp ups and downs that correspond to American perceptions. The U.S. no longer holds a position of strategic superiority over the Soviet Union, but this, as even Henry Kissinger once suggested, has little to do with day-to-day foreign policy. There is, in short, little agreement between the real world—where America is supreme in almost every major category of weapon systems and military advantage—and the appearance of the situation, where politicians (and a few radicals as well) go out of their way to demonstrate the strength of the Soviet Union,

Certainly the present period is one in which the fear of the Soviet threat is, as usual, wildly exaggerated. It is an article of faith to the resurgent Cold Warriors in Washington that the Russians have both expanded the rate of their military build-up and have become more aggressive in their interventions into other countries. The Committee on the Present Danger has called the Soviet military build-up "reminiscent of Nazi Germany's rearmament in the 1930s," a sentiment shared by numerous high policy makers in both the Carter and the Reagan Administrations.[7] The statistics accumulated by conservative defense groups have been adopted lock, stock and barrel by the Reagan Administration. For example, speaking before the U.S. National Defense University in July 1981, Secretary of Defense Weinberger used highly controversial figures about the Soviet military—a doubling of "real" defense spending, a six-fold increase in strategic nuclear weapons delivery, a tripling of battlefield nuclear weapons, etc.—to argue that the Russians seek superiority over the United States. Even more disputable, Weinberger claimed that all this Russian activity took place "unchallenged in recent years by the United States,"[8] as if America had done nothing to upgrade its forces.

There is good reason to doubt all these claims. Before he became a key Congressional supporter of the MX missile, Congressman Les Aspin conducted a thorough study of the alleged Soviet military build-up during the 1970s which indicated that any comparisons of Soviet military spending to the extremely sharp and rapid Nazi military build-up were hogwash. Aspin found that "The expansion of Soviet military efforts has been surprisingly steady over time, with some minor fluctuations depending on the stage of weapons deployment and the deployment cycle the Soviet Union is in."[9] Not only has the CIA used comparison figures that deliberately exaggerate Soviet spending, but in addition, there is evidence—brilliantly compiled in a recent book by Andrew Cockburn—which shows that Soviet weaponry is often clumsy, unworkable, and inefficient, something the Pentagon would never claim.[10] And by 1983, the CIA retracted the earlier estimates of Soviet military spending as far too high.

Nor is there evidence that America in recent years has allowed its forces to deteriorate. It is true that the rate of spending decreased after Vietnam, but, as Aspin points out, while "The Soviets are failing to match our reduction of recent years,...they never matched our jumps of previous years."[11] Moreover, U.S. defense spending has been increasing in real terms since the late 1970s, and the introduction of new high-tech weapons has given U.S. forces much more firepower than they had in Vietnam. Beyond all these attempts to play the numbers game, it is questionable whether higher military spending can be equated with strength. The weakness of the U.S. was manifested to the world when its defense budgets were exceptionally high during Vietnam. Indeed there is now evidence, compiled by writers like Mary Kaldor and James Fallows, which suggests that huge defense budgets contribute to gadgetry, not to effective defense.[12] For whatever it is worth, the record is clear: both superpowers spend enormously on the military (Reagan's performance is an exception to this trend); neither increases its sums drastically in a one or two year period; neither decreases its military spending; both find the translation of military spending into an effective foreign policy extremely difficult.

Not only is the charge of a rapid comparative gain in Soviet military spending simply not true, neither is the idea that the Russians have become more "adventurous" in their foreign interventions. Since the end of World War II, the Soviet Union and the United States have both jockeyed for more favorable positions in the Third World. Sometimes one country gains advantages and sometimes it loses them. In the last few years, according to the resurgent Cold Warriors, the Soviets have taken the upper hand in this competition; they point to Angola (where Cuban troops were active), Ethiopia, Afghanistan, and Iran as evidence of this new aggression. (This point of view is shared by some on the left who argue that without Soviet help, Third World revolutions would be doomed to fail). But the case for a hyperactive Soviet Union simply does not hold. True, the Russians were especially brutal in their invasion and occupation of Afghanistan, but Third World disputes are nearly always local in nature, as the U.S. discovered in Vietnam (and the Russians have learned in Kabul). More significantly, the Russians not only "lost" China, but have suffered defeats in Egypt, Somalia, and wherever they have meddled far from their borders. Revolutionaries, like those in Nicaragua, try to avoid the Soviet model as much as possible and rely on the Soviet Union not out of preference, but out of necessity. The complete inability of the Soviets to intervene on the side of Syria during the Israeli invasion of Lebanon demonstrated to the world how unreliable an alliance with Russia can be. In other words, the Soviet Union, which is, after all, a nuclear superpower, will attempt to shape global events as much as it can, but it is, if anything, less successful in recent years in achieving its goals than more.

Instead of examining Soviet foreign policy to understand America's fluctuating attitudes towards its antagonist, I will argue that we need to grasp certain peculiar features of American domestic politics. After World War II, the U.S. became a global superpower, determined to exercise its influence wherever possible around the world. Yet even though a Pax Americana was perfected, most Americans also wished to retain an ingrained skepticism toward world affairs. Americans, as many historians have emphasized, have long brought a quality of moralistic innocence to foreign policy.[13] In the postwar period, fear of the Soviet Union tapped important roots in America's political culture. By blaming all difficulties on the Soviet Union, America could have it two ways: it was possible both to perform as an imperial power determining the fate of other people, yet at the same time to act as if America were the aggrieved party, acting defensively to save the world, not offensively to control it. Anti-communism, in this case taking the concrete form of worrying about the Soviet threat, became the bottom line of American political rhetoric and action.

Fear of the Soviet Union, in short, began to dominate American politics at the point at which America became a global superpower. There were few ways in which the Soviet Union in any meaningful sense threatened the security of the United States after World War II. The results of that war, it seems clear in retrospect, left the Soviet Union a major power in Europe, but left the United States a major power in every area of the world, including Europe. Although an accommodation with the the Soviet Union would not have been easy to reach given that country's suspiciousness and its own ambitions, some agreement could have been reached with them had America been concerned solely with its security. But American policymakers in the immediate postwar period, though speaking the language of national security, had more global ambitions. They wanted the United States to become the dominant hegemonic power in the world. Given the residue of American isolationism and anti-imperial traditions, such an ambitious objective could never have been brought to fruition without a concerted effort to instill fear and hysteria into American attitudes toward a society which not only had geostrategic ambitions of its own, but was also ideologically repugnant to America's quasi-religious belief in capitalism. Although the United States had been anti-communist since even before the Russian Revolution, the Soviet threat was literally "invented" by American foreign policy managers to prepare domestic public opinion for America's new imperial role.

As soon as the Soviet threat began to dominate American politics, some unexpected consequences began to reveal themselves. Members of the foreign policy elite such as George Kennan, whose own powerful writings helped more than any other to solidify fear of the Soviet Union, began to recognize that the instrument they had devised was far too blunt. Before World War II, American liberals had tended to be interventionists and activists in foreign policy, while conservatives leaned toward isolationism. As the East Coast foreign policy establishment, symbolized by Kennan, Dean Acheson, and others influential in the Truman Administration, began to speak the language of the Soviet threat, they discovered that right-wing demagogues would be in a position to criticize them for not being anti-Soviet *enough*. Moreover, once the dust settled from World War II and the Soviet Union and the United States were entrenched in their respective areas of influence, it became obvious to the foreign policy elite that negotiation had to replace confrontation if the world were to be managed with some stability. Finally, as both superpowers began to develop nuclear weapons, it became even more clear to liberal members of the foreign policy elite that the simple-minded platitudes they once used to rally support for the empire had become contradictory to the goal of imperial management.

Yet what is easy to turn on is often excruciatingly difficult to turn off. American conservatives were not prepared to give up rabid anti-communism so easily, and the industrialists, unions, intellectuals and universities that found profit in the military budget tended to agree. In other words, once the Cold War locked into its pattern, the American foreign policy establishment was split in two over its views toward the Soviet Union. Both groups sought an American imperial hegemony. Both would use the Soviet threat when it served their purposes. But one viewed the Soviet threat as an occasional helpful tool to win Congressional and public support for a global foreign policy, while the other became ideologically committed to an ongoing, increasingly confrontational, and phenomenally expensive military build-up. The major question confronting American foreign policy in the postwar years, in short, was not whether the United States would be anti-Soviet, but which of two models of anti-Soviet attitudes it would utilize.

The factors which influence the choice of contrasting uses of the Soviet threat are more complicated that they first appear. It is commonly argued by many on the left that capitalism demands both heavy military expenditures to sustain itself and a global empire that can absorb domestic contradictions. It therefore follows, given this line of reasoning, that the Soviet threat is a product of the elite's need for markets and stable conditions throughout the world. Yet some of the most famous names in American capitalism— Rockefeller and Harriman among them—are active proponents of detente and Soviet trade,[14] while the strongest possible ideological opposition to the Soviet Union comes from social democrats and intellectuals close to the labor movement. Moreover, that part of the foreign policy establishment with ties to multinational corporations leans toward a more moderate "Trilateralist" perspective on the Soviet Union, while the more competitive and West Coast branches of American capitalism take the hard-line view. Finally, the deficits that follow from heavy military spending are enormously worrisome to financial capital, leading it to be cautious in advancing some of the more hysterical versions of the Soviet threat.

From a strictly economic standpoint, in other words, one might predict a *diminishing* in the intensity of the Soviet threat in American society. Having established America's imperial ambitions by cultivating the Soviet threat in the late 1940s, the foreign policy establishment would begin to relax, looking for expanded trade and responding to European fears that the Cold War was getting out of hand. This was exactly the case throughout the late 1970s, when the Trilateral Commission was influential in American life. It seemed, for a time, as if the Cold War was, to all intents and purposes, over. To be sure, both sides would periodically make nasty noises about the other. But the U.S. no longer made any serious effort to undermine Soviet control over Eastern Europe, and the Russians accepted a divided Berlin and American hegemony in its own spheres of influence. *Realpolitik* was then in fashion, symbolized by the SALT talks and detente, which reflected an effort by both superpowers to divide up the world between themselves. In other words, if America were a capitalist society pure and simple, imperial ambitions and macroeconomic considerations might easily have led to a decline in anti-Soviet hysteria, replaced by some kind of join U.S.-Soviet management of world affairs.

But America is not a capitalist society pure and simple; it is, politically speaking, democratic. And, ironically, it is precisely this relatively open political structure which, in my view, is responsible for the persistence of the more extreme version of the Soviet threat in American life. Some degree of anti-Soviet hostility would be inevitable in the United States, given both the unattractive and often oppressive nature of Soviet foreign and domestic life, combined with America's own global designs. But the answer to the question of why it is that some periods in postwar American history are far more anti-Soviet than others demands not an economic but a political explanation. In this book I will argue that in order to understand why at certain points fear of the Soviet Union pervades all aspects of American life, one would be mistaken to look only at the Soviet Union. (It will be clear from the text that I have little sympathy toward the Soviet Union and its foreign policy, but at the same time, I do not view my distaste for the Russians as an excuse to justify what the Americans do.) Americans filter their attitude toward the world through lenses that heavily overemphasize domestic considerations. I will argue that U.S. perceptions of hostile Soviet intentions have increased, not when the Russians have become more aggressive or militaristic, but when certain constellations of political forces have come together within the United States to force the question of the Soviet threat onto the American political agenda. This is as much true of the Reagan military build-up as it is of previous periods of Cold War anxiety. The rise and fall of the

Soviet threat, in a word, cannot be understood without reference to such matters as the American political party system, the dynamics of electoral campaigns, bureaucratic politics in the Pentagon, rivalries between different branches of government, and disputes within the elite over economic planning and foreign policy options.

If there is a domestic political explanation to the rise of the Soviet threat, there is also one for its fall. As American politics stablizes, previous fears of Soviet adventurism give way to concern about the possibility of war. Americans tend to be both extremely belligerent and extremely afraid of military adventurism at the same time. Indeed, one could, without exaggeration, claim that the dominant approach of the American people to the world is fear: when that fear is of Russians, military expenditure and intervention predominate; when that fear is of war, isolationism dominates. Having made clear to the politicians their enormous fear of the Russians, Americans are now also making clear their fear of war, threatening to change the balance of U.S. politics away from the rapid military build-up and extremely belligerent rhetoric of the early 1980s.

There is one extremely important reason to emphasize the domestic political basis to the rise and fall of the Soviet threat. If American capitalism requires extreme hostility to the Soviet Union in order to function, which in my opinion it does not, then there can be no peace between the superpowers until capitalism is overthrown—which, at this point, seems rather a way off. To some degree, of course, there will continue to be a threat of imminent war so long as there is so much profit and power to be gained by preparing for it. But waiting for the perfect day to arrive does not strike me as a particularly efficacious strategy for dealing with the mind-boggling plans of nuclear war strategists that are being put into operation at this very moment. American democracy is far from perfect; indeed, I shall argue in this book that it far too often causes more belligerence than would otherwise be the case. But it is also an opportunity, an opening through which popular pressure can be brought, not at this point to abolish war, but at least to foil the plans of those who seem determined to fight one. There is a long term and a short term agenda. In short term, a concerted effort to use the same democratic process that exaggerates the Soviet threat in order to undercut it seems to me work enough for one generation. No question will be more important to America's future than the question of the Soviet threat. And no question demands more stringently that we throw off the hysteria and wild claims that accompany it in order to find the underlying dynamics in the hope of reversing them.

CHAPTER II

THREE PEAKS
OF HOSTILITY

The U.S. and the Soviet Union, although allies during World War II, have been wary of each other since the Russian Revolution. This wariness broke out into active hostility when World War II ended, and it has continued ever since. Nonetheless, in spite of a constant fear of the Soviet Union in American politics since 1946, it is possible to identify differences in the way that the Soviet threat has been perceived for the past thirty-five years. In an influential study of the Cold War, for example, Daniel Yergin has made a distinction between what he calls the "Riga axioms" and the "Yalta axioms" about Soviet conduct. The former take the view that the Soviets are inherently bent on expansion, that the danger they pose constantly grows, and therefore that only firm U.S. resolve can meet the threat. (Yergin adopts the term Riga from the Latvian city from which Americans observed Soviet conduct before the U.S. recognized the regime.) The latter view, named after the city in which Roosevelt, Stalin, and Churchill achieved an understanding on the nature of the postwar world, sees the Soviets as a serious rival, but one that demands diplomatic responses through which each power tries to accommodate the interests of the other. The difference between the two interpretations is not that one is more sympathetic than the other to the Russians—both view the Soviet Union as an antagonist—but that the Riga position implies a military response, while the Yalta axioms do not make conflict the litmus test of U.S.-Soviet relations.[15]

Yergin's distinction is helpful in charting the rise and fall of the Soviet threat in American politics since the end of World War II. There have been certain periods of time in which, although much attention was paid to the evils of communism, the U.S. did not actively pursue a directly provocative course with respect to Russia. And there have been other times when a concern with Soviet perceptions of American weakness have led to a veritable obsession with "standing up to the Russians." One such obsession with the Soviet Union currently grips Washington policymakers.

For purposes of this study, a high peak in the perception of the Soviet threat can be defined as having the following characteristics. First, some important group of policymakers, in an official or quasi-official forum, issues a report making a claim that the Russians are getting stronger and the Americans weaker. This report is then read and debated in the highest circles of policymaking, fashioning a new consensus about the Soviet danger. As a result of the new perception, certain steps are taken to demonstrate America's concern. The two most important indications of the new mood are a decision to increase the defense budget and a decision to demonstrate U.S. strength in some way, either through a direct intervention or through a symbolic display like moving the American fleet. Both kinds of action are meant by policymakers to prove American resolve. Therefore, a peak in the perception of the Soviet threat requires a conjunction of an ideological offensive (as manifested in some new official statement about the rivalry between the two superpowers) combined with a manifest shift in policy toward policies that tangibly demonstrate a firmer course.

Contrariwise, a dip in the perception of the Soviet threat would occur when either the ideology or the action was missing, or both. For example, if the actual defense budget remains constant or decreases, and at the same time if the actual number of times that the U.S. "shows the fleet" declines, then such a period would not be an anti-Soviet peak, even if the ideological hostility toward the Soviet Union was strong. For our purposes, a trough in the hostile perception of the Soviet Union will be considered a period in which an anti-Russian ideology did not correspond with a palpable rise in foreign policy belligerence to produce a new U.S. offensive in the world.

Based upon these criteria, postwar American policy has gone through three peaks and two valleys. These periods can be identified as follows:

1. *The first peak:* the period of the cold war initiation. Right after World War II ended until the early 1950s, a very negative

interpretation of Soviet conduct began to win out in the United States. As a result, the basic decisions that began the Cold War—such as developing the H-bomb—were made.

2. *The first valley:* the Eisenhower retrenchment. In spite of all the anti-communist rhetoric of John Foster Dulles, ideology did not correspond with action under Eisenhower. The defense budget did not increase and U.S. foreign policy actions designed to prove America's resolve to the Russians were relatively few.

3. *The second peak:* the Cold War consolidation. Beginning in the late 1950s with the Gaither Report, a number of defense specialists began to question the Eisenhower approach. The anti-Soviet ideology was carried forward but to it was added, especially between 1961 and 1962, a new American belligerence in foreign affairs, culminating in the Cuban Missile Crisis.

4. *The second valley:* detente. Starting fitfully in 1963 with Kennedy's American University speech and continuing into the Nixon Administration, big-power cooperation began to increase. By the mid-1970s the defense budget (as a percent of GNP) had decreased, foreign interventions, while more blatant, were less numerous, and SALT I was signed and ratified.

5. *The third peak:* Carter to Reagan. Two years into the Carter Administration, just as a new strategic arms treaty with the Russians was concluded, a new wave of anti-Soviet hostility swept Washington. Ratification of SALT II became impossible. Pressures to increase military spending, especially after the Iranian hostage crisis and the Soviet invasion of Afghanistan, became irresistible. In such an atmosphere, the strong rhetoric of Ronald Reagan seemed a tonic, leading to the election of a conservative president and the attempt to put into practice some of the more extreme anti-Soviet perceptions available in the United States.

By reviewing the features of each of these periods in greater detail, it becomes possible to see what the peak points have in common—and what differentiates them from the valleys—in order to begin to unravel the domestic factors that combine to produce extreme domestic perceptions of the Soviet threat within the United States.

The Cold War Begins (1948-1952)

The issue that dominated policy discussions within the United States after World War II ended involved more than anything else the correct *perception* that the U.S. should have of Russian behavior. When the Yalta agreements called for free elections in Eastern Europe at the earliest possible time, for example, Stalin interpreted them to mean that the Soviets would be allowed a free hand in Poland, whereas Americans were sure that they meant that the future of that country was up for grabs. The Yalta agreement, as Truman's chief of staff Admiral William Leahy pointed out, "was susceptible to two interpretations."[16] As Stalin moved to consolidate Soviet control over Poland, the question became which interpretation would be the official American position: was Stalin's move to be perceived as acceptable under Yalta, or as the breaking of a treaty requiring a firm American response?

Secretary of War Henry L. Stimson and General George Marshall argued that the U.S. should be cautious in interpreting Stalin's moves because Russian cooperation was essential to the United States. Truman rejected that advice and turned instead to Leahy, whose antipathy toward the Russians was well known. Leahy called a meeting of high State Department officials known to be hostile to Stimson's and Marshall's interpretation of Soviet conduct. "It was the consensus of opinion of the conferees," Leahy wrote in his diary, "that the time had arrived to take a strong American attitude toward the Soviets, and that no particular harm can now be done to our war prospects even if Russia should slow down or even stop its war effort in Europe and Asia." Having thus chosen a negative interpretation of Soviet behavior, Truman met with Soviet Ambassador Molotov and proceeded to abuse him (and his country) verbally. "I have never been talked to like that in my life," Molotov exclaimed. "Carry out your agreements and you won't get talked to like that," was Truman's response.[17]

Hostility toward the Russian ambassador, however, was not something around which a diplomatic policy could be built. Policies are based, not only on the actions of other countries, but on how those actions are interpreted. The importance of the 1946-50 period was that, whenever it mattered, the U.S. opted for an interpretation that emphasized the globally aggressive character of the Soviet Union over equally plausible interpretations that stressed the other country's more narrow pursuit of a limited self-interest.

For example, when Truman sent Harry Hopkins—Roosevelt's most trusted advisor—to Moscow in the summer of 1945, Stalin was found to be reasonable, interested in possible attempts at cooperation, and even willing to compromise over Poland. The discussions were so frank and open that the two countries began to feel that they understood each other much better. This understanding continued for a time after Truman appointed James F. Byrnes as his Secretary of State. Conservative, Southern, Irish Catholic, and relentlessly ambitious, Byrnes felt that an accommodation with the Russians made good political sense. While in Moscow in late 1945, he negotiated a compromise with Stalin over Eastern Europe, won agreement for a United Nations Atomic Energy Commission, and worked out plans for Asia. There seemed to be no question that diplomacy with the Russians worked as diplomacy generally works: slowly, compromisingly, ambiguously, and peacefully. Yet all this evidence of the possibility of cooperation with the Soviet Union would be ignored as American politics turned increasingly in a Cold War direction.

Obvious points of tension and disagreement existed between the Russians and the Americans over such matters as Trieste, Iran, and reparations. Distinguished Americans like Marshall, Stimson, Hopkins, and Byrnes had all shown that it was possible to resolve some of those tensions through diplomacy. But within the United States a different lesson was being emphasized. Rejecting all evidence to the contrary, influential individuals and organizations began to argue that tension was the rule and cooperation the exception. The Russians, it was claimed, were an aggressive and totalitarian power bent on world conquest, and their ambitious schemes could be foiled only by American resolve. If Stalin refused to negotiate, that proved the point. And if he did negotiate, it merely showed how untrustworthy he was. Constructing a mindset from which all evidence could be shaped to fit their negative image of the Soviet Union, these officials were successful at undermining the efforts of Stimson and Byrnes. A hardline position began to emerge at home.

One faction that was instrumental in solidifying the hard line was the Russian desk of the State Department. For years Russian affairs had been in the hands of a generation of would-be patricians who aped the crumbling aristocracy of Europe. Joseph Grew, Loy Henderson, Eldridge Dubrow and others—all of them pompous, anti-semitic, tolerant of Hitler, elitist, anti-democratic, and ultra-reactionary in their politics—used every opportunity at their command to win a confused Truman around to their hard line views on the Soviet Union.[18]

Truman was receptive to the anti-Soviet views of the State Department. But those views became dominant only because a number of groups were willing to listen to extreme denunciations of Soviet conduct for their own reasons. Prominent Democrats like W. Averill Harriman and Dean Acheson were convinced that a firm anti-Soviet position would counter the vulnerability of their party in the conservative environment of the postwar period. Representatives of the Navy and the Air Force, trying to gain bureaucratic turf for themselves, saw in the Soviet threat a chance to score points against the Army. Liberals in the labor movement saw an opportunity to gain respectability and to wage war at the same time against radical antagonists, many of whom belonged to the Communist Party and thus could be painted with the anti-Russian brush. Industrialists with pro-European inclinations saw a chance to forge a close alliance between Germany—just recently the enemy—and the United States. Keynesian economists thought that the high military budgets associated with the Soviet threat would continue economic recovery and avoid another depression. In short, domestic interests were coalescing in such a way as to give currency to an extremely reactionary view of Soviet intentions that gained force and momentum due to factors above and beyond what the Soviets were doing.

In spite of the broad domestic coalition that was finding coherence around the notion of a Soviet threat, the idea of Russian expansionism was not immediately accepted, either within the elite or among the general population. Skeptics had to be converted by a sustained campaign to win support for one particular, and highly biased, interpretation of Soviet motives. Initially George Kennan, a career diplomat and the State Department's leading expert on Russia, took the lead in developing this point of view. First in a long telegram from Moscow and then in a 1945 article published under the name of "Mr. X" in the semi-official journal, *Foreign Affairs,* Kennan argued that Soviet imperialism was based on the Russian national character. If Kennan was correct in his analysis, then no compromise with the Soviets was possible, for they would not be satisfied until their way of life prevailed throughout the world. Kennan later came to regret the monomaniacal view of Soviet intentions that shaped U.S. politics but he clearly bore some responsibility for it, since his analysis left policymakers little option but to take the most anti-Soviet position possible. Kennan would not be the last policymaker who used anti-Soviet rhetoric only to be overtaken by more extreme positions that left him isolated.

The crest of anti-Soviet thinking in this initial wave of belligerence took the form of a study group organized by the Departments of Defense and State in 1949 to ponder the implications of Soviet possession of the atomic bomb. Eventually producing a position paper for use within the National Security Council called NSC-68, the study group painted a horrifying picture of Soviet desires. The nub of the argument was that an unbreakable connection existed between totalitarian conditions at home and an expansionist foreign policy abroad. "The Kremlin's policy toward areas not under its control is the elimination of resistance to its will and the extension of its influence and control. It is driven to follow this policy because it cannot...tolerate the existence of free societies; to the Kremlin the most mild and inoffensive free society is an affront, a challenge and a subversive influence. Given the nature of the Kremlin, and the evidence at hand, it seems clear that the ends toward which this policy is directed are the same as those where its control has already been established."[19] NSC-68, in other words, denied that the Russians could ever act like all other big powers, seeking to maximize their strength in some places and minimize their losses in others. Diplomacy means choice; by that definition, diplomacy with the Soviet Union was out of the question because they could never choose—their internal character would drive them to expand everywhere. NSC-68 analyzed Russian intentions in terms of a model of totalitarianism based on Nazi Germany. That the Soviet Union was a different social system in a different historical period was a distinction passed over by the emerging anti-Soviet consensus.

NSC-68 was never officially adopted by the Truman Administration, but it is generally viewed as a turning point in American policy because it provided the rationale for two major transformations. First, it called for programs which would triple the defense budget. Spurred by the Korean War, the defense budget did, in fact, shoot up. And since much of the newly expended money went to Europe, upon which NSC-68 had concentrated, and not Asia, where the war was actually taking place, the authors of the document were vindicated. Second, NSC-68 had a major impact, if an indirect one, on public opinion. Although it was a highly classified document seen only by a few, its intention, in the words of Dean Acheson, "was to bludgeon the mass mind of 'top government' so that not only could the President make a decision but that the decision could be carried out."[20] After NSC-68, dissenters within the Establishment who wished to articulate an alternative view of Soviet intentions had a far more difficult time winning a hearing. Now more united, the elite would convey the impression of the Soviet threat with greater clarity to the American people.

Thus, the period between the end of World War II and 1952 qualifies as a peak in anti-Soviet hostility because it meets the two criteria outlined above. First, an ideological offensive was undertaken against the Russians, one that emphasized the most negative features of Soviet activities in an ambiguous context. And second, this ideological offensive was combined with a more active foreign policy stance, particularly in an increase in defense spending oriented toward Western Europe.

An Official Perception of the Soviet Union

The Kremlin regards the United States as the only major threat to the achievement of its fundamental design. There is a basic conflict between the idea of freedom under a government of laws, and the idea of slavery under the grim oligarchy of the Kremlin, which has come to a crisis with the polarization of power described in Section I, and the exclusive possession of atomic weapons by the two protagonists. The idea of freedom, moreover, is peculiarly and intolerably subversive of the idea of slavery. But the opposite is not true. The implacable purpose of the slave state to eliminate the challenge of freedom has placed the two great powers at opposite poles. It is this fact which gives the present polarization of power the quality of a crisis.

This statement, and many others like it that are contained in NSC-68, indicates that to the men who wrote this document, there was a direct relationship between the authoritarian internal structure of a state and an external desire to expand. This notion, still advanced by anti-Soviet thinkers, is simply not true. Some democratic states have been highly expansionist, and some authoritarian ones (like Franco's Spain) have preoccupied themselves at home. Generally, states will become more active in foreign policy depending on their power in the world, not on their internal structure.

Retrenchment (1952-1957)

By 1950, a new hostile view of Russian conduct had emerged within U.S. policymaking circles. Yet even though the Soviet Union had replaced Nazi Germany in the American mind as the enemy, there still were significant obstacles to the adoption of the world view laid out in NSC-68. For one thing, most Americans thought of themselves as a peaceful people and were not prepared to engage their hearts and minds in a perpetual war after just having completed a global one. In addition, a state of vigilance against Soviet expansion required high defense budgets, which meant increased taxes, and Americans have never particularly liked to pay taxes. Finally, Cold War anxieties carried with them a domestic state of emergency, strong presidential powers, and an atmosphere of crisis—none of which seemed compatible with the overwhelming desire for normalcy in the postwar atmosphere. By electing General Eisenhower president, the American people selected a man who was not so prone to extreme interpretations of the Soviet threat. By 1952, the peak was turning into a valley, and a period of retrenchment began.

Eisenhower's Administration, like all of them in the postwar period, was staunchly anti-communist. The new Secretary of State, John Foster Dulles, was unbending in his opposition to communism, the kind of man who opposed sending a perfunctory telegram to the Russians on Stalin's death for fear that it might be interpreted as an incitement to revolution.[21] Dulles' self-righteous zeal colored the rhetoric of the Eisenhower Administration, but it did not control its policies. The fiscal conservatism of the Republican Party continuously acted as a constraint on U.S. policy during the 1950s, for any increase in defense spending was considered intolerable. Forced to practice what he called "maximum protection at bearable cost,"[22] Dulles was hamstrung in putting into operation some of his more extreme views. In the end, just six months from his death, even Dulles seemed to have second thoughts about his more inflexible notions. In mid-1958 he explored the idea of a partial military disengagement in Europe and seemed to endorse a reduction in tensions with the Russians.[23]

Thus, although the Eisenhower Administration possessed an ideological hatred of communism, it declined to mobilize an aggressive foreign policy against the Russians. (Anti-communism and anti-Soviet perceptions are not the same thing. Dulles, for example, seemed to be more hostile to the Chinese than the Russians, while some anti-Soviet belligerents—including members of the Reagan

Administration—are willing to form an alliance with a communist country like China.) For this reason, the Eisenhower Administration was missing one of the two elements that constitutes an extreme peak of anti-Soviet perceptions.

Neither an increase in defense spending nor an active interventionary stance designed to prove America's resolve characterized Eisenhower's foreign policy *actions*. In defense policy, the Administration repudiated the doctrines of NSC-68 and developed what it called the "New Look" in military strategy. The New Look, as Samuel Huntington pointed out, "was the special reflection of the values and goals of Dwight Eisenhower, George Humphrey, John Foster Dulles, Arthur W. Radford, their associates in the Administration, and the dominant groups in the Republican Party."[24] For this reason, it sought "stability of expenditures,"[25] not vast increases in new weapons systems.

A Russian Looks at Dulles

A word about Dulles. Dulles often said that the goal of the United States was to push Socialism in Europe back to the borders of the Soviet Union, and he seemed to be obsessed with the idea of encirclement. He extended America's economic embargo of the Soviet Union to include a boycott on cultural exchange. Not even Soviet tourists and chess players were permitted to visit the United States. I remember, too, that when the U.S. sponsored some sort of international convention of chess our own delegation wasn't allowed to attend.

However, I'll say this for him: Dulles knew how far he could push us, and he never pushed us too far. For instance, when the forces of our two countries confronted each other in the Near East during the events in Syria and Lebanon in 1958, Dulles stepped back from the brink of war. The reactionary forces of the United States and England pulled back their troops, partly as a result of Dulles' prudence. The prestige of the Soviet Union was enhanced in all the progressive countries of the world.

When Dulles died, I told my friend that although he had been a man who lived and breathed hatred of Communism and who despised progress, he had never stepped over that brink which he was always talking about in his speeches, and for that reason alone we should lament his passing.

from *Khrushchev Remembers*

Under enormous pressure from anti-Soviet ideologues, Eisenhower, as Huntington notes, held the line remarkably well; it was not until the very end of his Administration that the defense budget began to rise.

Nor, in this period of retrenchment, was there a significant increase in symbolic demonstrations of American power. Overall, Eisenhower's Administration saw a greater number of foreign policy adventures than Truman's (57 in 8 years, or an average of 7.1 per year, compared to Truman's 35 in 6 years, for an average of 5.8 per year) but a much lower number than Kennedy and Johnson (88 in 8 years or an average of 11.0 per year).[26] But the majority of these actions were not big power confrontations; they were more old-style interventions to help specific business interests (as in Guatemala) than new-style interventions designed to prove to the Russians that the U.S. was willing to flex its muscles. The Eisenhower people did not make every Third World revolution a "test of will" as the Kennedy team would do. Some of the major foreign policy problems of the Eisenhower period did not directly involve a U.S.-Soviet confrontation, especially the British attempt to hold on to the Suez Canal. Moreover, in spite of vast turmoil against Soviet rule in Eastern Europe, the Administration took no major steps to destabilize Russian power.

For these reasons, the anti-Soviet activists who had written NSC-68 became extremely disenchanted with the Eisenhower Administration, especially in the beginning of its second term. They began to organize themselves for a new offensive in developing a negative perception of Soviet conduct. There followed a second peak in cold war hostility as they came closer to holding power.

Cold War Consolidation (1957-1963)

The second peak in anti-Soviet sentiment began to form, as had the first, around a top secret review of Soviet capabilities. Called the *Gaither Report* after the review committee chairman, H. Rowan Gaither, *Deterrence and Survival in the Nuclear Age* reaffirmed the consensus that had been formed with NSC-68.[27] A simple chart captured the message of the report. With Soviet efforts plotted in a thick black line and the U.S. capacity in a thin one, the chart showed the U.S. ahead in the early 1950s, equality at the time the report was issued (1957) and a projected Soviet lead for the future. The Report also contained a point that would come back to haunt American policymakers; the authors claimed (falsely) that the Soviets soon would have enough intercontinental ballistic missiles to overwhelm America's defenses. In the strongest possible terms, the *Report* urged an immediate turn to high defense budgets and an effort to indoctrinate the public into a crisis mentality.

The *Gaither Report* was only one of the attacks on Eisenhower's New Look. Former Army Chief of Staff Maxwell Taylor (see Chapter V) led the public barrage with his book *An Uncertain Trumpet,* in which he called for a strategy of "Flexible Response" that, by building up conventional arms, would permit the U.S. to wield its forces more effectively.[28] The Council on Foreign Relations had sponsored a study by Henry Kissinger that argued

Past and Projected Relationship Between U.S. and U.S.S.R. Military Effort

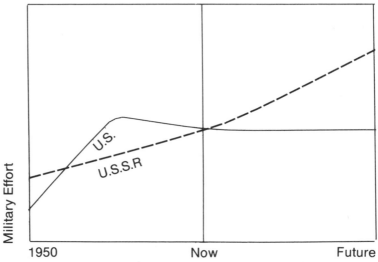

From: *The Gaither Report* (1957). The interesting point to note about this chart is that, even though it symbolized the kind of thinking that would have an enormous impact on U.S. defense policy, whoever drew the diagram would have failed an introductory course in policy analysis or economics. There are no figures given, the dates are vague, and the lines in the chart do not measure any empirical reality. In other words, the purposes of the chart were much more political than analytical. Nonetheless, it is a sign of the hysteria of the times that a chart this analytically weak could be taken seriously by anybody. It was the top secret nature of the Gaither Report that enabled such irresponsibility to take place.

much the same thesis, and also advocated planning for "limited nuclear war" so that the U.S. would not be bound by Dulles' reliance on big bombs.[29] Ambitious Democratic senators—like Stuart Symington of Missouri, John Kennedy of Massachusetts, Lyndon Johnson of Texas, and Hubert Humphrey of Minnesota (all of them candidates for president in 1960)—were attracted by the new wave of anti-Soviet sentiment, seeing in it a relatively safe way to criticize Eisenhower's complacency. If any of these men had been elected president in 1960 a more active U.S. stance in the world and higher military budgets would have been sure to follow.

Kennedy, the winner in this scramble, did not wait long. In his first year in office he increased the defense budget by 15%, putting most of the money into combat-related operations like Army divisions, the Marine Corps, and active vessels. He tripled draft calls, asked for the power to call up the reserves, and supported a civil defense program as a response to an announcement by Nikita Khrushchev that he was increasing Russia's defense budget. Paul Nitze and other authors of both NSC-68 and *The Gaither Report* were given high policymaking positions in the State and Defense Departments. Ignoring Eisenhower's by now legendary warning about a military-industrial complex whose "total influence...is felt in every city, every state house, every office of the federal governments," Kennedy gave free rein to his new Secretary of Defense Robert S. McNamara to make America's military might more "usable," that is, more able to be moved around the world to demonstrate America's willingness to control world events. (His support for "Special Forces" to be engaged in counter-insurgency warfare was a manifestation of this.) He let it be known that he would welcome a head-to-head confrontation with the Soviet Union, something that Eisenhower had tried to avoid. The Cold War was back, and in its revivified form, it was more confrontational.[30]

None of Kennedy's activism would have been possible without rekindling the image of the Soviet menace. Dean Rusk, the new Secretary of State, not only adopted Eisenhower's off-the-cuff remark about falling dominoes, but seemed to make it a principle of national policy. From now on, every conflict in the world, regardless of how far from home, would be seen as a supreme test of American resolve in the face of communist "aggression." (Rusk even linked Russia together with China, while a more perceptive statesman would have tried to exploit their differences.) A meeting with Khrushchev at Vienna produced no breakthroughs and was unable to patch up the hostility caused by the infamous U-2 incident. In the hostile world atmosphere that was the logical result of his "get tough" stance, Kennedy acted belligerently in Berlin (contributing to the construction of a wall that he was unable to remove), upped the U.S. commitment in Southeast Asia with consequences that would prove disastrous for the United States, and eschewed diplomacy over missiles in Cuba for a confrontation that left the whole world breathless with fear. Within two years, Kennedy had faced more foreign policy "crises" than faced Eisenhower in all eight of his presidential years.[31]

If evidence had existed that the Soviet Union had become palpably more aggressive, Kennedy's intensification of the Soviet threat might have been justified. But the evidence, as it usually is, was ambiguous. There can be little doubt that to at least some degree Khrushchev was testing the new president with bluffs and boasts. But boasting is not policy. If anything, Soviet foreign policy seemed to have become even more conservative since the death of Stalin. His first successor, Georgi Malenkov, tried to downplay military affairs in order to increase consumer spending within the Soviet Union. Even though Khrushchev played upon Russian military opposition to this approach to win their support, once in power he continued to favor an expansion of consumer goods. (The Russian leaders, like their American counterparts, have to worry about their popularity .) In 1956, Khrushchev repudiated Stalinism and relaxed Russia's hold over Yugoslavia and other Eastern European countries, though as those countries took advantage of their new found freedom, he backed off and reimposed Soviet control. Apart from the Soviet Union's blatant attempt to maintain its political control over Eastern Europe, its foreign policy was characterized by attempts to curry favor with the newly independent countries of the Third World (although it was not sure how) and a zig-zag between trying to find some sort of big-power cooperation with the United States and attempting to tweak its nose.

But despite such contradictory evidence of Soviet behavior, the new belligerents that came to power with Kennedy chose to ignore all evidence that did not conform to their fairly set view of Soviet expansionism. Their notion of a "missile gap"—which Kennedy had used effectively in his campaign—proved to be a lie; the Russians had less than a handful of ICBMs (one hand, not two) in 1960. Khrushchev had been bluffing, and moreover he was able to carry out his bluff over his own Cold Warriors by citing exaggerated U.S. estimates of Soviet strength. (We don't need any more, he told his generals, for look how many they say we already have.)[32]

Moreover, as was the case with the authors of NSC-68, the new Cold Warriors had a perception of Soviet intentions that was consistently negative. Refusing to understand the Soviet Union as a great power trying to maximize its interests in a world of great powers, they ignored nuance, took literally statements made for internal Soviet consumption, and tried their best to fit every Soviet action into a theory of communist expansion, whether the action had anything to do with the theory or not. Finally, the Kennedy people ignored evidence of internal splits within the socialist camp— such as the defection of Yugoslavia and the coming defection of China—because their mindset would not let them see its significance.

There is reason to believe that before he died, John Kennedy had come to understand the folly of his hard-line anti-Soviet position. In an unusually reasonable speech at American University on June 10, 1963, he spoke a new language, one stressing a search for areas of cooperation with the Soviet Union. He then forcibly pushed through Congress a test-ban treaty with the Russians which not only halted poisoning of the environment but also constituted a significant political defeat for dyed-in-the-wool Cold Warriors, who opposed the treaty until the end. Kennedy seemed to be making an effort to back down from the confrontation mentality that had brought him serious embarassment in the Bay of Pigs invasion. By 1963, the second wave of anti-Soviet belligerency seemed to be coming to an end.

Yet although Kennedy did take a few courageous steps to bring the Cold War under control, he also began the process that ultimately led to a U.S. defeat in Indochina. Both Kennedy and his successor Lyndon Johnson were determined not to expose themselves to the right-wing charge of being soft on communism. Accepting at face value the notion of an international communist conspiracy, they trapped themselves by their own rhetoric. Their view of the world made them escalate a nationalist struggle for independence in Vietnam into a major confrontation with both the Soviet Union and China, neither of which wanted it. China, as events would show, has traditionally been at odds with Vietnam. And the Russians, while supplying Vietnam with arms and with political support in the international arena, did everything they could to bring the war to an end, for they wanted above all else to stabilize the area. By the way it intervened in Vietnam, the U.S. was creating a self-fulfilling prophecy, forcing the socialist bloc countries to oppose its moves, thereby confirming American suspicion of Russian and Chinese "intransigence."

The period between 1957 and 1962 constitutes the second peak of anti-Soviet concern because it combined a new ideological offensive—*The Gaither Report* and the Taylor and Kissinger books—with deliberate actions like raising the military budget and increasing the number of direct U.S. foreign policy actions. Although nostalgia about the Kennedy presidency has somewhat obscured the fact, this period was also a time of extreme Cold War tension in the everyday lives of ordinary people: crises, civil defense, and brinks of terror. The Kennedy-Johnson Administrations were sympathetic to some of the most extreme anti-Soviet views floating around Washington and made them rationales for American policy.

How to be More Dialectical Than the Marxists

The Soviet Union watched the arrival of the new administration with marked interest. Khrushchev, who had given up on Eisenhower after the U-2 incident and the collapse of the Paris summit in May 1960, seized several opportunities to semaphore his hopes for Kennedy. His messages to Harriman and others after the election were followed by a Pugwash meeting on disarmament in Moscow in December. These gatherings, so called because they began with a conference called by the Cleveland financier Cyrus Eaton, at his summer place in Pugwash, Nova Scotia, brought together disarmament experts from both sides in supposedly unofficial exchanges. Walt Rostow and Jerome B. Wiesner, who were among the Americans at the Moscow meeting, saw V. V. Kuznetsov of the Soviet Foreign Office and urged the release of two American RB-47 fliers, shot down over the Arctic the preceeding July. In the course of their talk Kuznetsov mentioned the campaign furor about a 'missile gap' and suggested that, if the new administration went in for massive rearmament, it could not expect the Russians to sit still. Rostow replied that any Kennedy rearmament would be designed to improve the stability of the deterrent, and that the Soviet Union should recognize this as in the interests of peace; but Kuznetsov, innocent of the higher calculus of deterrence as recently developed in the United States, brusquely dismissed the explanation.

From Arthur Schlesinger, Jr., *A Thousand Days*

This passage perhaps says more about how Kennedy's advisors viewed Soviet credulity than it does about Soviet intentions.

Detente (1963-64; 1968-78)

The second peak had crested early with Kennedy's American University speech and attempts to negotiate a test-ban treaty, but because of the persistence of the war in Vietnam, a full-scale relaxation of tensions was impossible to achieve. It was not until the Nixon years that detente would become a reality.

Nixon's was hardly a pacifist administration. In his conduct of the war in Southeast Asia, as a devastating book by William Shawcross demonstrates, Nixon (and Kissinger) acted with extreme insensitivity, cruelty, and ignorance.[33] Moreover, both were adept at manipulating anti-communist symbols when it suited them to do so. Nonetheless, Nixon did begin to take the steps that would prove to the world that big-power politics works more effectively in the international system than ideological rigidity. In spite of the extreme anti-Soviet views of his Secretary of Defense James Schlesinger, Nixon's policies of detente with the Russians and his opening with China meant that the Cold War could not be carried on as it had been.

Nixon's 1972 China trip marked a watershed in U.S. politics, for it brought to an end America's longstanding attempt to pretend that the world's largest country did not exist. But from the point of view of anti-Soviet perceptions, it did not constitute a relaxation of tensions, for it could be interpreted as an anti-Soviet move. More significant for U.S.-Russian relations was the negotiation of the Strategic Arms Limitation Treaty (over the opposition of Democratic hard-liners). Nixon, even more remarkably, won approval for the SALT I treaty in the Senate and managed to have its provisions accepted by the Pentagon.[34] While it is certainly true that the SALT I treaty legitimated the arms race by creating high ceilings which each side then felt obligated to fill, there can also be no doubt that its approval meant a modification of the pattern of mutual antagonism between the U.S. and the Soviet Union. In this sense the most important product of detente was the intangible one, the sense that it was possible for two superpowers to find concrete areas of agreement so that each could look more at its own society rather than blaming the other for its problems. For this reason alone, Nixon accomplished more toward the relaxation of anti-Soviet perceptions than his Democratic predecessors.

Behind foreign policy decisions there generally lies a theory about nation states and how they behave. The Cold War had been motivated by a theory that had taken hold in policymaking circles which argued that because Russia was a totalitarian society, it was bound to expand as much as possible, forcing the U.S. to "contain" it (the Riga axioms). In order to bring about detente, Nixon and Kissinger were forced to discard this theory in favor of a "Yalta" mentality that would rationalize big power politics. It is worth a short digression to consider their approach.

Kissinger, schooled in the Germanic tradition of political theory, understood that power is inherently conservative. Leaders of countries (and of organizations), he believed, try to protect their privileged position and are inherently suspicious of any challenges to their authority. From this point of view, Kissinger quickly recognized that, whatever their respective ideologies, the U.S. and the Soviet Union were both powerful states that would operate as conservative forces in the world. Both had an interest in protecting themselves from challenges, whether (of concern to the Americans) from other capitalist countries like Germany, (of concern to the Russians) from other socialist countries like China, or (of concern to both) from instablity in the Third World. Kissinger argued that although there were many possible centers of power in the Third World, the U.S. and the Soviet Union together were so overwhelmingly powerful militarily that they could insure "stability." Rather than worrying about Soviet intentions—which in Kissinger's view just "confuse[s] the debate"—the U.S. should "discipline power so that it bears a rational relationship to the objectives likely to be in dispute."[35] While willing to bring up the Soviet threat for domestic purposes, Kissinger was not fixated on it.

These views were not necessarily "better" or more "moral" than those of the anti-Soviet hawks, but they were different. The clear import of Kissinger's *realpolitik* meant an end to the excessive ideological hostility between the two superpowers, and therefore fewer attempts to mobilize America's force around the world.

By the two measures being used in this study to represent foreign policy aggressiveness—increases in the defense budget and the number of shows of force—the Nixon period constituted a definite valley. Expenditures on national defense as a percentage of the Gross National Product showed the following pattern in the 1960s and 1970s:[36]

1966	8.0%	1971	6.60%
1967	8.98	1972	6.27
1968	8.85	1973	5.63
1969	8.16	1974	5.45
1970	7.48	1975	5.49
		1976	5.09

In short, fairly dramatic decreases in the percentage of GNP consumed by the defense budget took place under Nixon. Moreover, there was a similar drop in the number of foreign policy interventions. Although the Kennedy and Johnson Administrations had averaged 11.0 interventions per year, there were only thirty-three in the eight years of Nixon and Ford, for an average of 4.1.[37] In large measure, this reluctance to show force was due to the American popular reaction against Vietnam, which acted as a constraint on the ability of any administration to commit U.S. troops. But it also followed in part from the relaxation of the most extreme perceptions of the Soviet Union that followed inevitably from detente. Without a sharply negative view of an enemy, it is difficult to justify an activist foreign policy.

The Carter-Reagan Period: A New Peak (1977-?)

The policymakers who had produced NSC-68 and the Gaither Report understood that if U.S.-Soviet detente continued, the positions for which they had fought would be undermined. The anti-Soviet forces, early in the 1970s, began to regroup. Winning allies from within the Nixon Adminstration (like James Schlesinger, who was forced out of his position as Defense Secretary in a highly publicized dispute with Kissinger), Paul Nitze, Eugene Rostow, and other unreconstructed believers in the Soviet threat took steps to launch a new surge in anti-Soviet perceptions. Within just a few years, these men would come to power with the Reagan Administration.

Veteran's Day, 1976, three days after the election, was the date on which the Committee on the Present Danger held a news conference to announce its perception of "a Soviet drive for dominance based upon an unparalleled military buildup."[38] Issuing a none-too-subtle warning to the recently elected Jimmy Carter, the Committee set itself up as the guardian of the national interest. From a position outside the new administration, it would lead the crusade for a resumption of Cold War hostilities with the Soviet Union.

Behind the ideological fervor of the Committee was a host of statistics arguing that the Soviets had used the detente period to obtain military advantages (or near-advantages) over the United States. To support its case, the Committee—in opposition to

How to Organize a Cold War

National Strategy Information Center, INC
111 East 58th Street
New York, N.Y. 10022

Area Code 212 375-2912

May 24, 1976

Dr. Eugene V. Rostow
Professor of Law
Yale University
New Haven, CT 06520

Dear Gene:

Earnestly hoping for your acceptance, our Directors have authorized me to invite you to join our Board. (You should know that we've been granted $1 million to "crank up" an all-out effort to meet the current and growing threat from the USSR—whether in military, ideological or economic warfare terms.)

You are fully aware, of course, that in terms of the shifting military balance—and in our diplomatic credibility in much of the world—the U.S. today is about where Britain was in 1938, with the shadow of Hitler's Germany darkening all of Europe.

In this context, NSIC is opening a *full scale Washington office* to:

Kissinger's doctrine—retreated to the traditional Cold War view of Soviet intentions. For example, one of the leading intellectuals of the new offensive, Richard Pipes (a professor of Russian history at Harvard), wrote an article in which he claimed that the Russians were contemplating preparations for war with the United States.[39] (Pipes would later work for Ronald Reagan.)

In order to make the case for a Soviet threat to the United States—especially in the post-detente context—the new cold war-riors followed the now established pattern of commissioning a study group to report on the U.S.-Soviet military balance. For years, the C.I.A had been compiling estimates of the military capabilities of other countries, including the Soviet Union. Called national intelligence estimates (NIEs), these reports became the

a) interact with policy echelons in the White House and Pentagon (where we still have many friends);

b) "tutor" Congressional Staffs, and brief members;

c) work with Trade Associations—with an interest in "defense"—which have Washington offices;

d) generate more public information through friends in the Washington press corps who write about military and foreign affairs.

I, personally, will move to Washington in September to supervise our "interface" operation. (We will also continue our "educational" program, which now reaches 350 universities.)

Please join with us!

With best regards, I am

Faithfully
Frank R. Barnet

cc: Robert B. Burke
Frank N. Trager

P.S.: Inasmuch as I'll be in Europe May 15-June 17 (attending NATO "think-tank" sessions in six Allied nations), if you have any questions, please feel free to contact Dr. Frank Trager, our Director of Studies.

I think you have in your files most of our Publications and our basic brochure; but, if there's anything else you need to refresh your understanding of our program, please let us know.

official basis for strategic planning. Toward the end of the Ford Administration, an official NIE came under scathing criticism from some of the more extreme anti-Soviet policymakers involved in the process. (One of them, retired General Daniel Graham, said that "there are more liberals per square foot in the CIA than in any other part of the government.")[40] As a response to this criticism, President Ford, in the spring of 1976, appointed a group of outsiders to review the NIEs. This study group, known as Team B, included men like Richard Pipes, Paul Nitze, and other members of what would become the Committee on the Present Danger. The Team B report was predictable. It argued that the previous NIEs had been wrong, that the Soviets were engineering a massive build-up in order to pressure the West, and that a major U.S. response was

---

How to Organize a Cold War (contd.)

YALE UNIVERSITY
Law School
New Haven, Connecticut

June 1, 1976

Eugene V. Rostow

Mr. Frank R. Barnet
President
National Strategy Information Center, Inc.
111 East 58th Street
New York, New York, 10022

Dear Frank,

I am honored to accept your invitation of May 24 to join the Board of the National Strategy Information Center. I am delighted that you are opening a Washington office to conduct a campaign of direct and large scale persuasion to Congress, the Executive Branch, Trade Associations and the press corps.

On the political and political-military side, as you know, our new Committee on the Present Danger, of which you will be an active member, is planning a comparable if more limited operation. It should be no problem to coordinate our activities and indeed to act jointly on many issues.

---

needed. The Team B report was to the 1970s what the Gaither Report had been to the 1950s and NSC-68 to the 1940s.[41]

Team B was only part of the picture of increasingly hostile perceptions of Soviet intentions. Articles in *Commentary*, effective lobbying by the Pentagon and private think tanks, Republican Party assertiveness, and attempts to mobilize the Cold War faction of the Democratic Party combined to produce a new wave of belligerency. But would the new wave turn into a peak? That depended on both the Russians and the policymakers within the Carter Administration.

Jimmy Carter began his presidency seemingly determined to continue the detente that had shown such positive results for Richard Nixon. During his campaign the new president had warned against an inordinate fear of communism and had prom-

I fully agree, as you know, with your estimate that we are living in a pre-war and not post-war world, and that our posture today is comparable to that of Britain, France and the United States during the Thirties. Whether we are at the Rhineland or the Munich watershed remains to be seen. I won't quarrel with your dating!

I assume that you see the Strategic Review, which reprinted a speech I gave in New York last January. Do let me know if you do not have a copy.

Yours cordially,

[Gene]

The Honorable David Packard
The Honorable Henry H. Fowler
The Honorable Paul Nitze
Mr. Charles Tyroler
Max M. Kampelman, Esq.
The Honorable Charls Walker
Professor C.B. Marshall
Richard Allen, Esq.
Mr. Lane Kirkland
The Honorable James Schlesinger
The Honorable Rita Hauser

ised to cut military spending, which did not endear him to the Committee on the Present Danger. Indeed, Carter avoided the Committee entirely when he appointed his staff, preferring instead the more moderate views of Wall Street bankers and Trilateral intellectuals. (The appointment of anti-Soviet hardliners like Zbigniew Brzezinski and Samuel P. Huntington was an exception to this trend). As pressure on the Administration to pursue a more anti-communist foreign policy increased, Carter tried to balance the views of "doves" like Cyrus Vance and "hawks" like Brzezinski. Marshall Shulman, Carter's main advisor on the Soviet Union, said that the U.S. should seek both competition and cooperation with the Russians, which reflected the internal debates within the Administration but was irrelevant to the hurly-burly of domestic politics.[42] No clear-cut position on the nature of the Soviet threat emerged during the early Carter years.

The confusion surrounding the Carter Administration's attitude toward the Soviet Union was expressed in Presidential Review
Memorandum 10, a document that was meant to rival NSC-68 and
The Gaither Report, but which achieved little because of internal
contradictions. PRM-10 has never been made public, but reports in
the press indicate that it was composed of two parts. One argued
that between the two superpowers there existed "essential equi-
valence" in nuclear weapons, which meant that neither could
effectively threaten the other by brandishing its strategic arms.
However, a second portion concluded that conflict between the
superpowers was still intense in certain key areas, especially the
Middle East, where conventional arms were important. The gist of
the report was that the U.S should concentrate its efforts to gain
superiority over the Soviet Union in Europe and the Middle East
while trying to preserve the precarious balance in nuclear weapons
that existed and would, in all likelihood, continue to exist. Written
in this way, PRM-10 was acceptable to both the hardliners in the
Carter camp like Samuel Huntington and Zbigniew Brzezinski and
to the critics of cold war extremism like Paul Warnke and his aide,
Lynn Davis. In this sense, PRM-10, like NSC-68, had as much to do
with domestic political controversies as it did with the actual state
of the world.

The longer the Carter Administration stayed in office, the
more precarious became its middle-of-the-road approach to the
Soviet Union. In part, Soviet behavior was responsible, for the
Russians, after making inroads in Ethiopia and Angola, in December 1979 sent troops into Afghanistan—which Carter inflatedly
called the greatest threat to peace since World War II—and seemed
to profit from the Islamic revolution in Iran. Yet as the elections of
1980 approached, domestic factors that shaped perceptions of the
Soviet threat intervened as well. Just as Maxwell Taylor had once
organized internal opposition to the policies of Eisenhower, men
like Paul Nitze, excluded from office under Carter, began to agitate
against the administration. Neo-conservatives within the Democratic Party were too strong for the president to ignore; it is now
almost forgotten, but during 1979 the Carter Administration
played up a Russian threat in Cuba, led by the desire of liberal
Senator Frank Church to win reelection. As organizations like the
Committee on the Present Danger intensified their criticisms of the
administration, Carter seemed to back away even from his own
SALT II treaty, despite support for it from former President Ford.

Carter increasingly saw himself as Harry Truman, warning of a new crisis and calling for increases in defense spending. The Administration read the same polls as everyone else; military spending was popular once again, and Jimmy Carter moved to cover the popular ground. Under Reagan it is easy to forget that the latest peak of Cold War sentiment most assuredly began under Jimmy Carter.

The intentions of the Russians in 1979-80 could be read many ways. There was no question that the Soviets acted unilaterally in Afghanistan and were taking advantage of whatever situation they could. But it was also clear that the Kremlin was strongly committed to SALT II, much more committed than the U.S. Senate. When the SALT treaty was delayed to overlap with the election campaign in the U.S., its chance of passage evaporated. SALT— technical, obtuse, unpublicized—was too easy a target for political opportunism. Elections tend to bring out the most simple-minded analyses, and when that happened, the path was smoothed for Ronald Reagan, a candidate anxious to forgo complexity for cliches. SALT became a dirty word, and the fact that it was Carter's treaty worked against him in the campaign. (In reality, all politicians, including Reagan, knew that SALT II was a good deal for the Americans, and its provisions are still, to this day, observed by both sides, even though certain basing modes for the MX missile, if adopted, would violate the treaty).

When Ronald Reagan was elected president, anti-Soviet hostility reached a new peak easily comparable to the immediate postwar period and the Kennedy missile crisis. The new president claimed that a 3% "real" increase in the military budget, which Carter advocated, was not sufficient, and he used his considerable powers of persuasion to commit the United States to unprecedentedly high peacetime levels of military spending. Under Ronald Reagan every single attribute of previous Cold War revivals played a rerun: civil defense, emotional vigilance, scare publications, inflated rhetoric, fears of intelligence breakdowns, spy stories, restrictions on information, sanctions on the Soviet Union, new weapons systems, military confrontations, threats to intervene in Latin America, black-and-white stereotyping, revivals of American patriotism, and an attempt to force U.S. allies to conform to a foreign policy that they increasingly saw as against their interest.

As I indicated in the previous chapter, the Reagan Administration carried its preoccupation with the Russians to the most extreme point in modern U.S. history. Unlike any previous president, Mr. Reagan said, and then said over and over again, that the

Russians were ahead of the United States in all categories of weapons development—an assertion that all of Washington knows privately is completely untrue. Because he refused to soften his rhetoric about Russian intentions, Secretary Weinberger created unprecedented discord with American foreign policy in Europe and brought about a Congressional revolt against a major weapons system—the MX missile with a dense pack basing system. (The MX was later salvaged after a presidential commission linked its fate to arms control talks with the Russians and to the development of a smaller missile called the Midgetman, but even with this brilliant political move, the fate of the MX was still udcertain). In short, as the tenor of American politics swung back again from the hysteria of 1980, the President remained committed to a mandate that no longer existed, still blaming the Russians for every evil in the world even though the U.S. economy was in bad shape due to the deficits incurred by heavy military spending.

And so it went. As if detente had never existed, as if Europe were still threatened by Soviet troops poised to march, as if the Third World had never tried to find a new course, as if the economy could support endless spending on the military without regard for cost, as if inflation had never been stimulated by war expenditures in the 1960s; as if, in short, the world was in exactly the same place as it had been in 1948, the Reagan Administration was determined to place the least favorable, most hostile attitude toward the Soviet Union at the core of its approach to the world. Detente was dead, the Cold War, now for the third time in thirty-five years, had returned, and a new administration seemed committed to doing everything in its power to keeping it there.

From this review of the peaks and valleys of anti-Soviet sentiment since World War II, it becomes possible to make a few tentative conclusions.

First, while anti-communism is a more or less permanent feature of American politics, anti-Soviet perceptions have gone through distinct phases. Each increase in hostile perceptions has certain similarities. A group of officials or intellectuals—generally of a conservative persuasion—will make a strong case for adopting a more hostile interpretation of Soviet conduct over a more ambiguous one. Moreover these generally right-wing views (although they are often associated with Democrats who take a "liberal" position on the domestic issues as well) create an atmosphere in which it becomes difficult for the incumbent president to ignore the increasingly hostile perception. Then, as a result of the new consensus, concrete acts—such as an increase in the defense budget or a foreign policy intervention—express the new hard-line position. The record shows that while the right-wing view of Soviet intentions never changes, what does change is the seriousness with which that view is taken within an incumbent administration.

Second, it begins to become clear that anti-Soviet perceptions reach a peak, not because certain policymakers intentionally engage in a campaign to redirect foreign policy (although some try to do this), but because various constellations of forces come together to give more negative perceptions of the Soviet threat greater credence. Political convenience rather than conspiracy produces a Soviet scare.

Third, a strong case can be made that the peaks of anti-Soviet hostility are not directly related to increases in the Soviet Union's "aggressiveness." To be sure, there is evidence of Soviet advances for each period of cold war hostility: Eastern Europe, especially Czechoslovakia, for the first peak; Cuba for the second; and Afghanistan for the third. But it is difficult to discover a cause and effect. There has been a long history of conflict between the U.S. and the Soviet Union. *The real issue is not whether the Soviets become more aggressive, but whether the U.S. decides to view them as more aggressive* (and vice versa). For example, much evidence existed at each anti-Soviet peak to support an opposite interpretation of Soviet motives: postwar cooperation and signs from Stalin that he wanted to negotiate in the late 1940s; the change in the regime and decision to downplay military spending in the 1950s, combined with Soviet willingness to negotiate a test-ban treaty; and deliberate Soviet restraint in Vietnam, Iran and the Middle East combined with an overwhelming desire to conclude a SALT II treaty in the 1970s. U.S.-Soviet accommodation over the postwar period is fully as impressive as the antagonism between them. *What needs to be explained then is why, when the evidence is always ambiguous, the more negative perceptions develop at the time they do.* Specific Soviet actions have something to do with the answer, but we must look elsewhere for a full explanation.

Finally, if actions by the Soviet Union are of only tangential importance in understanding the rise and fall of the Soviet threat, then political events at home may well be more crucial. The question becomes whether it is possible to discover similarities in the three periods when anti-Soviet perceptions peaked and began to influence policy. If there are common features to all these periods, then one can conclude that domestic politics may be more important in explaining the Soviet threat than relations between the United States and the Soviet Union.

In the next five chapters, I will examine five domestic features that each of the peaks has, to one degree or another, in common. These include: the pattern of party politics; cycles of presidential strength and weakness; inter-service rivalries; debates over the locus of foreign policy; and patterns of economic growth.

CHAPTER III

THE CENTER CANNOT HOLD

The most striking features that all three peaks of anti-Soviet hostility have in common is that each began when the Democrats held the presidency. Does this mean, as Senator Robert Dole charged during the 1976 election campaign, that the Democrats are a war party? In some sense it does, but only because the Republicans force them to be. In order to understand the role that domestic politics play in raising the level of intensity of the Soviet threat, it is important to examine the way the two political parties treat foreign policy.

My argument in this chapter will be that hostile perceptions of the Soviet Union tend to occur under similar political conditions. First, a new president, generally a Democrat, assumes office. During this time, the right wing organizes itself around the notion of a Soviet threat, a politically safe issue for it since it is out of power and need not concern itself with putting new policies into effect. Pressure from the right makes the newly installed president vulnerable. If there was equally strong pressure from the left, in favor of programs oriented toward greater equality and a foreign policy permitting smaller defense budgets, the new president would not be forced to lean rightwards. But without a strong left, Democratic presidents invariably adopt a more aggressive foreign policy as a way of protecting their political base. This also gives them the appearance of being bold and decisive, which cuts down some of the need to adopt aggressive domestic programs—ones that would antagonize big business and conservative interest groups.

Eventually, the cold war fever that afflicts the Democrats spreads to the Republicans as well, until new fiscal or international realities bring anti-Soviet obsessions into more reasonable focus.

At the end of World War II there was a deep uncertainty about the form that American politics would take. The New Deal coalition of Franklin Roosevelt was no longer in an unchallenged position as conservative ideas became more popular. Starting late in the 1930s and then continuing through the war, business had fought strenuously to regain respectability in America. White Southerners, who had been part of a populist tradition at one point in time, were turning conservative in the face of the race issue. Isolationism, an important current in American political life with both Socialist and Republican roots, had lodged itself in the latter party as the former ceased to exist.

When he became president, Harry Truman was fully aware of the resurging conservative sentiment in the country. Without the personal magnetism that had enabled Roosevelt to survive, Truman had to make important political decisions, and he had very little time in which to do so. Most importantly, he had two options as he faced the right-wing thrust. He could, on the one hand, make an attempt to unify the New Deal coalition and face the right head-on. Such an approach meant moving to the left by mobilizing new constituents among the working class, minorities and women and fighting for new policies like medical insurance, housing, and extensions of social welfare. Alternatively, he could attempt to meet the right's challenge by co-opting it, moving in a conservative direction by restricting new constituencies and not being aggressive about new policies.

Either course meant risks for Truman. If he moved to the right, he risked disaffection from liberals. Business, the white South, and isolationists would not support a Democratic president without demanding a price, and in order to win their allegiance Truman would have to promise incentives to business, concessions to racism, and appeals to American nativism, none of which would please the inheritors of Roosevelt's progressivism. Yet if Truman moved to the left, he would allow the demagogues that were rising throughout the land to smear him with being soft on everything. No wonder that Truman tried his hardest to avoid a choice. He searched desperately for a position in the center, one that would forestall the extremes from both directions and enable him to build a new political coalition. In this he was successful, for in the postwar period a new centrist political coalition did come to power, one that has dominated the Democratic Party—and therefore

America—for a generation. This coalition has been called "Cold War liberalism" or alternatively, the politics of domestic and overseas economic growth.[43] The Cold War liberal coalition included business, labor, intellectuals and the military. The building of this remarkable growth coalition could never have been achieved without one essential ingredient: the fear of the Soviet threat.

Anti-communism was capable of working like magic in containing both the right and the left versions of how to organize America. Business, for example, had traditionally opposed using government as a stimulant for the economy. Rejecting Keynesian economics as subversive, most American businessmen—with the exception of far-sighted groups like the Committee on Economic Development—felt that increased government activity would mean higher budgets and higher taxes. For the economic activists around Truman, this opposition presented a dilemma: how could they involve the state in macroeconomic management without antagonizing business sentiment? High defense budgets solved the problem: they would be used to stimulate the economy without invoking opposition from the right. While Truman personally remained unconvinced—he called for limits on the defense budget and, even when he approved increases, he demanded that they be "stretched out"[44]—the political logic of the situation overwhelmed the President. Before Truman's presidency was over, the defense budget had become an economic stimulant. And when the new money was spent in the South and West, it also brought Southerners and former isolationists into the coalition. In this manner, the military budget ultimately became the unifying force that prevented the right from setting itself up in successful opposition to the new centrist consensus.

At the same time, anti-communism did not necessarily have to alienate the left. True, the Marshall Plan and the foreign policy of containment would mean that a small segment of the left—the one that united around Henry Wallace and the Progressive Party— would venture out on its own. But by adopting progressive issues like housing and health care (even while restructuring them in ways that would win some business support), Truman was able to preserve his symbolic links to the New Deal and to minimize his losses. Meanwhile, other segments of the left would support him fully in his newly discovered anti-communism. Those liberals who had fought against the Communist Party (and often lost) could ride the wave of anti-communism and obtain their revenge. Union leaders like Walter Reuther, ambitious politicians like Hubert Humphrey and Paul Douglas, intellectuals in the Americans for

Democratic Action—all were as strongly anti-communist as the Republicans.[45] They could be counted on to be enthusiasts for the centrist course and to mobilize the voters and write the platforms that would sustain it. But, once again, there could be no successful attempt to win this segment of the liberal community—and to isolate the more radical Communist Party and its sympathizers—without making some strong claims about the danger that Russia posed.

Besides this magical political quality of the Soviet threat, broad agreement in the center of the political spectrum gave U.S. foreign policy an apolitical quality, as if it had nothing to do with partisan strife but was a unified response to an external enemy. For most of the postwar period, American foreign policy has been described as bipartisan, a process that began in the late 1940s when President Truman won support for his initiatives from Senator Arthur Vandenberg. Because Vandenberg was a Republican and a conservative, his support for Truman undercut the potentially powerful right-wing opposition to an active foreign policy. Foreign policy was therefore thought to be "above" partisan strife.

Yet bipartisanship from the start was inherently partisan. While liberal Democrats may have prided themselves on how cleverly they co-opted the right, in actuality they paid a high price, for they were forced to become more conservative and bellicose in order to keep the right's support. In effect, it meant that if the Democrats adopted the Republican's hyperbole, the Republicans would charitably restrain their criticism. Thus was a certain pattern established. First, a conservative Republican would wonder aloud whether the U.S. was doing all it could to remain the number one military power in the world. Then a Democratic president would assure the nation that, yes, we were as strong as we could be. Having approved a few new weapons systems, sponsored an increase in the defense budget, and intervened somewhere around the world, the Democrat would obtain assurance from the conservative critic that, yes indeed, we seemed to be on the right track. In this matter, bipartisanship insured that debates over national security policy would always be skewed sharply to the right. (Yet, it seems not sharply enough: in 1979, the Republicans officially repudiated bipartisanship, to enable them to criticize the Carter Administration even more harshly than they did Truman, Kennedy, or Johnson.)

Given all these currents, it is no wonder that the Soviet threat became such an important feature of American politics after World War II. International political events clearly were an aspect of cold war hostility, but one simply cannot ignore the internal dynamics of U.S. party politics in trying to understand why the more negative perceptions of the Soviet Union were accepted over alternative images. Moreover, American party politics continued to influence domestic perceptions of the Soviet threat. In a few short years, debates over the direction of American foreign policy abruptly stopped. Neither the isolationist right nor the progressive peace lobby could win a hearing for its point of view as the cold war liberal coalition came to dominate the political spectrum.

Secure in its hegemony, cold war liberalism was the lifeblood of the Democratic Party in the postwar period. In consequence, all postwar Democratic presidents have found themselves in the position of being forced to adopt negative perceptions of Soviet conduct. John F. Kennedy, for example, faced a potential stalemate similar to Truman's. Barely elected, and with the conservative bloc strong in Congress, Kennedy had little room for political maneuvering. Substantial segments of his own party distrusted him, either because they viewed him as an illegitimate heir to Adlai Stevenson or because they were suspicious of his urbane cosmopolitanism. The Republicans saw in his election an opportunity to increase the belligerancy that had become central to their role in the bipartisan process. In short, for all his talk about activism and idealism, Kennedy's hold on political power was precarious.

Kennedy and his advisors were convinced that the public was far to the right of themselves, and therefore they were wary of doing too much. But at the same time, Democrats claim that the Republicans are the "do nothing" party, and in order to distinguish themselves from stand-pattism, they have to do something once in power. Torn between the need to do something and fear of doing anything, Kennedy was left with the traditional course of waging full scale battles against universally recognized enemies. Primary among these was the Soviet Union. From the moment of his Inaugural—when he called for increases in air power, the building of nuclear missiles, and the development of the Polaris submarine—to the end of his presidency, Kennedy sought to expand the military budget. And his advisors searched the world to find a place where the new military might could be demonstrated. For Kennedy, the answer to his domestic political dilemma was to be aggressive around the world, and thus to rekindle the fear of the Soviet threat.

In retrospect, there was an air of inevitability to the resurgence of negative images of the Soviet threat in the early years of the Kennedy Administration. If, in a democratic society, domestic pressures shape foreign policy responses, then the only direction in which the Administration could move was to the right. By 1960, whatever remained of the left had disintegrated. First, the anti-communism of the Truman period and then McCarthyism had wiped out radicalism as an effective force in American life. Then the Eisenhower years had worshipped a benumbing apathy that left little place for controversy and dissent. While the seeds of the civil rights movement were planted in the late 1950s, no significant opposition to the assumption of a global foreign policy on the part of the United States was able to make itself felt. Without anything to fear on the left, Kennedy had to worry only about the right. His belligerency toward the Russians protected that flank. Thus, so long as he kept alive the Soviet threat, Kennedy had a relatively clear field to himself. An aggressive foreign policy therefore became a crucial link in his governing coalition.

Lyndon Johnson, who inherited so much from Kennedy, inherited the mantle of cold war liberalism as well: indeed Johnson became the single most conspicuous example of the tendency to fight external enemies and internal social problems at the same time. Johnson, unlike Kennedy, pushed for and obtained a path-breaking legislative program. In so doing, he destroyed one of the central myths of American politics, that the country is so conservative it would never support changes in its political practices. On the contrary, Johnson's efforts showed that with an aggressive platform and with a favorable legislative majority, movements in a leftward direction were feasible. Yet having stretched the realm of the possible in domestic life, Johnson narrowed it in foreign policy. Rather than drawing the conclusion that the right was a paper tiger, he fell into the traditional Democratic fear of a rightwing backlash. Certain that his Great Society left him exposed to the Neanderthals, Johnson did everything in his power to prove how aggressive he could be overseas, first sponsoring the invasion of the Dominican Republic and then ruining his own accomplishments by persevering in Vietnam. Had Johnson carried over into foreign policy the lessons of the Great Society, he would have broken the cold war liberal pattern, liberated the Democratic Party from its need to exaggerate the Soviet threat, and conceivably have become one of the greatest of American presidents. Instead he was forced to retire in disgrace.

If the peaks of anti-Soviet hostility have certain political features in common, so should the valleys. And indeed, just as the former are dominated by Democrats pursuing Cold War liberal policies, the latter are dominated by Republicans with a different domestic political agenda. The Republican Party, at the presidential level, did not have to face the same kind of domestic dilemmas that bedevil liberal Democrats. Eisenhower, for example, simply was not as vulnerable to the right. It is true that the right, in the form of Senator Joseph McCarthy and his allies, did try to attack the General, but the notion that such a conservative man as Eisenhower could be "soft" on communism was so ludicrous that this tactical mistake began McCarthy's downfall. Nor did Eisenhower face any pressure from the left. The debates between activist idealists and realistic powerbrokers on the left had been won so handily by the latter that all the Democrats could do was to accuse Eisenhower of not being anti-communist *enough*. Immune to the need to build a domestic governing coalition, Eisenhower therefore had no particular interest in choosing the most hostile possible interpretations of Soviet conduct. Such domestic freedom gave Eisenhower's foreign policy enormous potential room to maneuver, although the president chose not to exercise his potential very much. A genuinely conservative administration did not need the image of a hostile Soviet threat in the same way that a would-be conservative one did.

Nixon and Kissinger were in a similarly favorable position. Nixon hoped to fashion an "emerging Republican majority" by uniting the white working class of the North with conservatives in the South and West over a strategy of trying to roll back the social gains experienced by minorities during the 1960s. To accomplish this task, Nixon did need foreign policy bellicosity, but he could rely on largely symbolic anti-communism for domestic consumption while searching for big-power accommodations with the Soviet Union. Highly symbolic foreign policy militancy works better for Republicans than for Democrats, for the latter's vulnerability to the right means that they often have to combine actions with words. The former, because they are the right, find that words suffice to shore up their domestic image of "toughness." So long as he reduced U.S. troop levels in Vietnam, Nixon was free to do most of what he wanted in foreign policy. It was not detente that disgraced him, but his own domestic arrogance.

Thus, by 1976 we can see a clear pattern emerge, in which the shape of domestic political coalitions clearly has an impact in determining whether an administration will choose a highly negative image of Soviet conduct, leading to confrontation, or a big power view, leading to some form of accommodation. This same pattern continued under the presidency of Jimmy Carter, but with consequences that would add a new, and more dangerous, twist to the role that partisan politics played in exacerbating the Soviet threat.

Jimmy Carter, like Kennedy, assumed power after eight years of Republican rule. Moreover, his predecessor, like Kennedy's, had taken actions that reduced the level of tension in the world, however shortsighted he may have been in other areas. Under Nixon and Kissinger the most negative images of the Soviet Union had receded substantially. By relaxing the Cold War, Nixon performed an invaluable service for Carter. He did what no Democrat could ever do, which was to prepare the groundwork for some reasonable order in the world. As a result of Nixon's and Kissinger's endorsement of detente and because of their support for a strategic arms limitation treaty with the Russians, the anti-Soviet Cold Warriors were isolated for the first time in the postwar period. In this way, Nixon put Jimmy Carter in the position of being the first postwar Democratic president who might not *need* the Cold War. Whenever the hawks began their attack, which they were certain to do, Carter had a possible response; he could claim that he was merely following the principles of his impeccably anti-communist predecessor. Carter, had he been a more courageous politican, might have used bipartisanship to protect himself from the Cold Warriors in the right wing of his party, just as "moderate" Republicans had used the concept in the late 1940s to protect themselves from the extreme right of their party.

Courage, however, was essential, for no Democrat could govern his own party by practicing politics as usual. By the time that Carter had assumed office, the length and intensity of the Cold War had transformed many key features of American politics. Although Truman's support of Cold War policies had associated with it opportunistic aspects, by the late 1970s many Democrats had come to accept the Soviet threat as an indispensible part of their outlook on the world. Defense plants, hawkish labor unions, support for Israel and macroeconomic stimulation had all combined with the power of military men, contractors, and spies to produce a firm coalition in favor of increased defense spending and a renewed foreign policy militancy. Senators like the late Henry Jackson and Daniel Patrick Moynihan, former policy makers like Paul Nitze and his friends in the Committee on the Present Danger, and columnists like Joseph Kraft were leading the chorus in favor of a Cold War coda. Carter, like his Democratic predecessors, faced the question of which path to take, but, unlike them, he had less margin for error, given his lack of political gumption.

Jimmy Carter made the assumption that Cold War sentiment could be effectively bought off through compromise and symbolic gestures, an assumption which failed to take account of the intense, indeed the fanatical, quality of the resurgent Cold Warriors. Instead of coopting anti-Soviet hysteria, Carter's decision to appear tougher with the Russians simply intensified it, so that the more that Carter moved to the right, the further right the discourse shifted. Thus because Carter felt that he had to endorse the MX missile for domestic political reasons—his Administration clearly recognized that the missile had no workable basing mode and would not, in any case, close the "window of vulnerability" that was alleged to be its rationale—he created an atmosphere in which the life of a thoroughly dangerous and quite unnecessary missile system was allowed to be extended. Similarly, when Carter called for a building-up of the defense budget after events in Iran and Afghanistan disturbed the public consciousness, he was constrained by the fact that, since he was in power, his target could never meet the more extreme calls coming from those who, out of power, would not have to find a way to pay for all the new weapons systems. In short, while a centrist position cemented by the Soviet threat had existed for Truman, enabling him to contain the right, by the time Carter became president the same tactic of lurching toward the center emboldened the right.

The net effect of the Carter presidency was to undermine thoroughly the appeal of detente and to lead to the election of a Republican far more sincere in his articulation of the Soviet threat than Carter. When Ronald Reagan became president, a new stage in the relationship between domestic politics and foreign policy perceptions was reached, for under previous Republicans like Eisenhower and Nixon, Cold War hysteria eventually subsided, whereas under Reagan it reached unprecedented new heights. Does this mean that the historic relationship between Cold War perceptions and Democratic presidents has become obsolete? It would, in my opinion, be an error to jump to that conclusion too quickly. Instead we should try to understand the significance of the Reagan electoral victory in the context of postwar party politics.

Ronald Reagan put together a package of appealing programs in his presidential campaign of 1980. One thing this package was conspicuously *not* was traditional Republicanism. In both domestic and foreign policy, Reagan ran against the historical legacy of his own party. His domestic notions, emphasizing supply-side tax cuts, bore much closer resemblance to deficit spending proposals than they did to the orthodox Republican belief in balanced budgets. And in foreign policy Reagan avoided an isolationist and cautious approach to world affairs in favor of an active and aggressive foreign policy that had been more associated with Democrats than with Republicans. Indeed, in its basic essentials—rapid economic growth at home and an equally rapid expansion of military capacity abroad—the Reagan agenda was closer to the platform of John F. Kennedy than to any other previous postwar incumbent. Americans, especially during periods of international crisis, have liked candidates who offer to increase national security; at one time those candidates had tended to be Democratic, but by 1980 they had become Republican.

This suggests that 1980 did represent a watershed election in recent American history, but not because, as commonly supposed, it signified the rise of the right. Reagan's agenda was, in its economic and foreign policy aspects, in accord with the pattern of postwar politics, not in violation of it. (His views on women, social issues, school prayer, civil rights, and evolution, however, did constitute a brand-new agenda). In 1980, in short, the same dynamics described in this chapter were working, but they had come to affect the internal dynamics of the Republican Party more than they colored the composition of the Democratic Party.

Once in office, Mr. Reagan found himself facing a party as divided as the Democrats had been when they were in office. (In a country as internally diverse as the United States, broken into classes, regions, and ethnic groups, a certain disunity has to be taken for granted.) As he faced fractious disputes over budgets that would not balance, economic policies solved inflation but accented unemployment and the necessity of raising taxes in order to avoid the disastrous consequences of cutting them, Mr. Reagan, like previous Democrats, longed for the world of foreign policy, where unity could be achieved around the need to draw closer together in the face of a common enemy.

Patterns of party politics, therefore, still influence the ways in which the Soviet Union is perceived in the United States. But the advent of the Reagan administration has created new aspects of the pattern that increase the instabilities of world politics. For one thing, the officials of the Reagan Administration, unlike those under Jimmy Carter, clearly *believe* in the Soviet threat. American foreign policy is being made by ideological missionaries who impose their world view in the fact of realities that speak otherwise, undermining confidence in Washington's ability to act in terms of the way the world actually is. Moreover, the Reagan Administration has failed to recognize—at least at the time of this writing—what all previous administrations were forced to acknowledge: no matter how much the Soviet Union is denounced for internal political purposes, when it comes to putting restraints on the Pentagon or negotiating treaties with the Russians, one must operate differently in private than in public. Previous presidents of both parties, whatever their rhetoric, signed treaties like the Anti-Ballistic Missile Treaty or agreements on chemical warfare which the Reagan Administration does not wish to preserve. Similarly, from Truman to Carter, presidents have ultimately found themselves at odds with the Pentagon, asking Congress, often quietly, to cut or slow up the military budget in order to bring fiscal sanity. To this point, the Reagan Administration, the most anti-communist in recent American history, has been unwilling to play by the generally understood rules. (In 1983, at a time of acute budget deficits, Secretary Weinberger asked for an astonishing 22% increase in defense spending; Republicans in Congress were as appalled as Democrats.)

If the Reagan Administration continues to pursue foreign policy based upon the most negative possible interpretation of Soviet conduct, one would expect the Democrats, as the party of opposition, to urge caution and restraint. If this were to take place, the entire pattern of postwar domestic input into foreign policy would reverse itself. However, there is reason to believe that the Reagan Administration may not be able to continue its hawkish foreign policy, in which case the future patterns of party politics will remain confused and uncertain.

Within one year after taking office, Ronald Reagan began to discover that his plans for a vast increase in military spending violated his beliefs in tax relief. Under fiscal pressure, the Reagan Administration rejected the lavishly expensive basing mode for the MX missile proposed by Carter, searching, sometimes desperately, for a cheaper solution. Furthermore, domestic political considerations forced Mr. Reagan—not once, but twice—to agree to wheat sales with the Soviet Union, hardly a satisfactory policy if one is convinced that they are trying to rule the world. Finally, America's allies in Western Europe, the very countries presumably in the front line of Soviet expansion, do not like the new Cold War and, to the degree that they continue to trade with the Russians, find themselves facing economic sanctions from the United States. Pressure from Atlanticist and NATO interests impose restraints on how anti-Soviet the Reagan Administration can be.

The effect of trying to put into practice some of the most extreme theories about Soviet behavior, in other words, has had the impact of undermining the solidity of the fear of a Soviet threat. In

1980 the American people were clearly scared and anxious to do whatever they could to meet the "challenge" from the Soviet Union. Two years later there was talk of a nuclear freeze, major disputes between the allies, New Right distrust of Ronald Reagan, pressure to stretch out or even postpone defense expenditures just recently approved, and a sense that the whole wave of insecurity about Soviet military spending and aggression may have been exaggerated. The Reagan Administration desperately wants to keep the third peak of anti-Soviet hostility at its height, but in spite of its best efforts, a relaxation of tensions may occur nonetheless. The reason for believing this is simple: despite the near-unanimous sentiment in the United States in 1980 that the Russians were conforming to Committee on the Present Danger stereotypes, the truth was otherwise. The great fear that propelled Ronald Reagan into office had domestic roots, and once those roots were exposed, the fear subsided. Soviet foreign policy had little to do with these matters either when the fear was great or when it began to calm down.

There are some Democrats, associated with the neo-conservative wing of the Party, who already feel that Ronald Reagan has softened and needs to be criticized from a more pure anti-Soviet threat position. If they take the leadership in future elections, we will return to the pattern by which the Democrats adopt the more Cold War positions. But a more likely scenario is that each party will be divided between its hawkish and less hawkish elements. The most extreme negative perceptions of the Soviet Union will unify both parties as they serve in opposition and campaign for office, but in the real world of limited funds, internal disputes within the Atlantic Alliance, the graying of Soviet leadership in the Chernenko and post-Chernenko era, and the changes taking place in Eastern Europe, no administration, of either political party, will be able to govern for long based on extreme Cold War stereotyped. That will be the ironic legacy of the Reagan Administration: to discredit the Soviet threat by believing it.

There will be those who will insist until their last breath that the reason why the fear of the Soviet Union became strong in the United States when it did was because of actions taken by the Russians. The increase in Cold War sentiment after 1976, they will argue, has nothing to do with Democrats and Republicans but is solely due to the fact that the Soviets are rapidly expanding their military capabilities and taking advantage of perceived American weakness by becoming more adventuresome in Africa, Afghanistan, and the Middle East. To be sure, the global power situation has changed in recent years. In particular, all advanced nations of the world have lost power, including the United States, as Third World revolutions and the rise of China to world power status have altered the nature of international relations. The U.S., without question, is no longer the unchallenged hegemonic power it once was. But it is anything but powerless at the same time and it retains its military and political superiority over a Soviet state which has also lost power in the world. Both superpowers are losing influence simultaneously. The Republican right, in other words, was correct to say that America was in worse shape, but incorrect to suggest that the Russians were in better shape. Domestic political patterns help explain why they made the latter charge anyway. Once Carter opted for Cold War politics as usual, instead of standing for a governing strategy that would seek to keep the loyalty of blacks, unions, women, and other such groups, then inevitably, a pattern of high defense budgets, fears of a Soviet military buildup, and opposition to detente and SALT were given prominent place in domestic debate, preparing the way for Reagan's political triumph.

From this review of the political features that the cycles of anti-Soviet belligerency have in common, it is possible to offer some thoughts on the conditions under which policymakers in America adopt a more negative perception of Russian intentions.

1. The Soviet threat has nearly always been more exaggerated under Democratic presidents than under Republican ones. The Democratic Party is, and remains, a Cold War party.

2. This does not mean, however, that the Democrats are to be blamed for the Cold War and the Republicans absolved. The former party becomes more belligerent only when it is egged on by the latter. Republicans concentrate, when out of power, on American weakness, for they have a domestic program that has never been very popular. Even though their ideas are often more symbolic than real, the Democrats take them seriously, more seriously than the Republicans take them themselves, and constantly try to put them into practice.

3. The main reason why alarmist perceptions of the Soviet threat do not go away, even when conditions demand that they should, is because of the absence of a strong left in the United States. Without a left that focuses attention on domestic needs, Democratic presidents have little choice but to turn to the right in foreign policy.

4. In the past, three features of the American political system—Republican opportunism, Democratic control over the policymaking process, and the lack of a strong left—combined to intensify

expressions of the Soviet threat. When one of these factors was missing—when the Republicans came to power, when the Democrats were in opposition, or as in the 1930s, when the left was strong—fear of the Russians declined in American politics. After 1980, this pattern has changed. The Republicans under Reagan have adopted the more extreme Cold War proclivities once associated with the Democrats. If this pattern continues, the roles of the two parties may reverse. But a more likely possibility is that the pursuit of extreme Cold War programs against the Soviet Union will become difficult, leading to the possibility that the third peak of cold war sentiment will transform itself to a third valley. In any case, it seems unlikely for the pattern by which the fear of the Russians rises and falls to be altered substantially until one of the other political party decides to rethink its commitment to a politic of overseas attention as a substitute for domestic reconstruction.

CHAPTER IV

THE PRESIDENCY
AND ITS ENEMIES

After Vietnam and Watergate, many observers think of a strong presidency as being responsible for some of the abuses in the American political system. Yet there is a peculiar way in which the peaks of anti-Soviet hostility correspond, not so much to the strength of the presidency, but to it weakness. In this chapter, I will set forward the proposition that high points of anti-Soviet perception correspond with attempts by presidents to defend the power of the office against attacks upon it.

Much of American ideology is sympathetic to weak government, but the American economic system since the latter part of the nineteenth century has demanded a strong one. Traditionally, therefore, there have been cycles in which activist presidents have expanded the power of the presidency, only to see its power watered down in later years. In the period since World War II, there have been a number of occasions when power seemed to be passing away from the presidency, commencing a cycle of weak executive power. It has been precisely during those periods when negative perceptions of an external enemy heightened, and one consequence was to preserve presidential power.

Over the long historical sweep of American life, the fear of centralized political power has never gone away.[46] So long as America was a rural society, its anti-government bias did not interfere with the serious business of living one's life as best as one could. But the growth of a national economy required expanded national governance, and eventually that expanded governmental activity encouraged the growth of the executive branch, the only branch capable of coordinating it. When the Great Depression hit America, the need for a strong state increased, and it increased even further as foreign and military policies assumed a position of unchallenged prominence in American life.[47] An intense longing for small and simple government was in conflict with a national and international need for a powerful and centralized executive branch.

The result was a deep contradiction at the heart of American political life. On the one hand, the specific political and economic features of a modern political economy—giant corporations, an expanded state that served their needs with huge public construction projects, a welfare state, and a global foreign policy aimed at stabilizing the world's markets—all demanded an active, strong executive. On the other hand, popular ideology, the Constitution, local elites, and competitive sector businessmen all preferred a weak central government and a passive executive. There was no way to reconcile these two demands. As a result, American politics have been characterized by a cyclical pattern in which activist presidents like Theodore Roosevelt and Woodrow Wilson strengthened the executive but were immediately followed by others who relaxed presidential power and passed it back to the states. Until World War II, every single increase in presidential power brought forth a decrease later on.

When Franklin Roosevelt died and was replaced by Truman, a reaction against presidential power set in. From the states, from Congress, and from the heartlands of America came demands to simplify life, to return power to the people, and to reestablish normality. For example, Truman's globally oriented advisors were telling him how important it was to retain some U.S. troops in Europe in order to maximize American leverage there after the war ended. But so strong was the demand for a more normal existence that Truman was effectively prevented from so doing; the troops came home. This experience with demobilization made it clear to presidential activists (like Clark Clifford) that unless steps were taken to curb such sentiment, all the gains that had been made by the executive since 1932 might be lost. Without a strong executive, men like Clifford reasoned, the U.S. would be unable to exercise world leadership; its role in the world's markets would be undermined by foreign competition; its welfare state would be in danger; and the entire political coalition that had brought the U.S. out of the Depression and had fought the war would fall apart.

Republican electoral victories, first in 1946 and then in 1948, had made the Congress, particularly the Senate, the locus of the cyclical attack on presidential power. The old-fashioned American right-wing Republicans were arguing that a global foreign policy was a cover up for presidential dictatorship, a device for insuring the domination of the economy by internationally-oriented, monopolistic American firms. As the right wing became stronger, Truman's ability to preserve a strong presidency became weaker.

The rise of a negative perception of Soviet conduct must be seen in light of these debates over presidential power. This is not to argue that policymakers deliberately exaggerated the Soviet threat in order to keep the executive strong, although there is evidence that on two occasions, to be discussed momentarily, such specific intentions were present. But it is to suggest that the entire atmosphere associated with the fears of an external enemy is conducive to making the argument for strong presidential power seem more valid.[48]

One case of a fairly deliberate decision by the Truman Administration to adopt a negative perception of Soviet conduct in order to protect the presidency came over the Truman Doctrine. Truman's advisors had convinced the president that securing public support for aid to Greece and Turkey demanded an "all out" speech portraying Soviet activities as a major threat to the security of the United States. To do so would be to ignore evidence that events in both countries were local in scope, the result of long historical forces, and not a result of Soviet "aggression." Two of the most prominent Soviet specialists in the United States, George Kennan and Charles Bohlen, both strongly anti-communist, blanched when they saw a draft of Truman's speech because of its provocative overtones. Their objections were overruled on the grounds that in order to win Senate approval of a new foreign policy (the Senate was attracted to isolationism and was wary of giving up its role in foreign policy, as an aggressive new doctrine like containment would force it to do), a militant anti-Soviet speech was essential.[49] Thus Cold War perceptions were cultivated, not because of international affairs, but because of domestic political conditions.

A more extreme example of the deliberate cultivation of anti-Soviet perceptions in order to protect the executive branch against its enemies came over Berlin, the hottest seat in the Cold War. In 1948 the U.S. was shocked when a cable arrived from General Lucius Clay, commander of American forces in West Germany, painting Soviet aggression in such strong terms that men like

Kennan felt a war to be in the offing. Later, after the damage had been done in terms of both solidifying American distrust of the Soviet role in Germany and confirming the Russian view of American aggressive tendencies, Clay admitted that he had sent his cable for domestic political reasons in the U.S. "Its primary purpose," wrote the General's biographer, "was to assist the military chiefs in their Congressional testimony; it was not, in Clay's opinion, related to any change in Soviet strategy."[50] American policymakers were apparently willing to risk war in order to prevent Congress from reasserting its power over the decision-making process. In such ways the downswing of the cycle away from executive power that would have "naturally" occurred was prevented and under Truman the executive was able to hold onto its prerogatives in the face of a general distrust of the executive branch.

Yet these are extreme examples, not representative of general trends. In most cases, the relationship between negative perceptions of the Soviet Union and decisions to preserve presidential power are more the result of a coincidence of interest than they are directly intentional. It tends to be the case that those presidents who are most in need of an active foreign policy in order to hold together their governing coalition (see Chapter III) are those presidents who accept as essential the need for a strong presidency as a solution to domestic and foreign needs.

John Kennedy, for example, began his campaign for the presidency convinced that Eisenhower had done the U.S. a great disservice by not being a sufficiently aggressive executive. In the early 1960s, Kennedy rejected a "restricted concept of the Presidency," and said that the nation's leader should become "the vital center of action in our whole scheme of government." Moreover, Kennedy seemed to endorse unconstitutional actions, at least to those conservatives who take a restricted reading of the Constitution, when he said that the President should be "prepared to exercise the fullest powers of his office—all that are specified and some that are not."[51] At the time, these seemed like progressive sentiments. To some degree they were, for Kennedy (at some point down the road) wanted to extend those trends that broadened the welfare state and protected civil liberties. But, as would soon become clear, his notion of an expanded presidency also meant unchecked foreign interventions and the cultivation of a sense of permanent crisis.

Kennedy practiced what he preached. During his administration tendencies toward concentrated power increased. Distrustful of the State Department, Kennedy placed responsibility for foreign affairs in the hands of a few men on his personal staff. Those men generally showed contempt for Congress' role in foreign policy, reaching a high point when Nicholas Katzenbach, a Kennedy aide who stayed on to work for Lyndon Johnson, told Congress that it could just go ahead and impeach the president if it did not like what he was doing. This distrust of all agencies of power outside the presidency was characteristic of both the Kennedy and the Johnson Administrations. For them, highly dramatic foreign policy crises, requiring decisive presidential action, added to the glamour of their Administrations, and also worked to still any thoughts that Congress, local elites, conservative defenders of the Constitution, or ordinary people might have about a simpler political system in which the president did not have such awesome power. Both Kennedy and Johnson found themselves comfortable with a foreign policy stance that was activist and, because it was activist, maintained the necessity of strong presidential power.

No president undermined the power of the executive more than did Richard Nixon through his clumsy attempts to expand it. Although a strong executive had in the past been favored by Democrats and opposed by Republicans, Nixon confounded the pattern by expanding presidential power in order to pursue conservative goals. It was a master stroke. Liberals detested the ends but admired the means; conservatives were enraptured by the ends but distrusted the means. Neither side, therefore, was in a position to criticize Nixon for what he was doing. Had Nixon successfully carried out his conservative *coup d'etat*, he would have realigned American attitudes toward the question of presidential power.[52]

The Watergate scandal was thus both a boom and a bust to the believers in an active presidency that congregated around the Democratic Party. It disgraced Nixon and opened the way for the Democrats to reoccupy the White House. But at the same time, Nixon had given a bad name to presidential power, and a strong executive was still central to the practice of the Democratic Party, since advanced capitalism, the welfare state, and global ambitions were still very much on its mind. At the height of Watergate prominent Democrats were trying desperately to make a distinction between executive power—which was good, and Nixon's power—which was bad. Joseph Califano, who would become Jimmy Carter's Secretary of Health, Education and Welfare, insisted that "a strong presidency is essential to the future of this nation and the freedom of our people" and implied that Nixon had failed not because he had too much power, but because he had too little.[53] The biggest challenge facing the Carter Administration was how to restore the legitimate authority of a strong presidency after both Vietnam and Watergate had reawakened the traditional American desire to fracture political power and keep it weak.

Carter was not very successful at this task. Despite his best efforts to transform the energy crisis into the "moral equivalent of war," skepticism of emergencies had been too firmly ingrained in the American people to produce much of a response. When Carter discovered the Cold War, making hair-raising speeches about Soviet intentions such as one at Wake Forrest College in 1978, he seemed mechanical and unconvincing, as if reading lines written for others. Carter increasingly began to see himself as a 1940s figure, defending the West against threat from the East, but distrust of his motives, and questions about his competence prevented him from playing the traditional strong presidential role of Democratic activists. Carter had close advisors, especially Zbigniew Brzezinski, who shared Kennedyesque conceptions about presidential power, but they never really took hold. Compared to the fervid language of earlier periods the Russian menace was invoked in an obligatory fashion, almost apologetically, as if Carter had no other vocabulary for speaking about the world.

As a result of Carter's inability to rally the country around stirring presidential leadership—an inability, in fairness to Carter, that can also be attributed to just plain public exhaustion after years of crisis—the third peak in anti-Soviet hysteria did not follow the same script of the previous two. If anything, America's latest flirtation with the idea of a Soviet menace was inspired by Congress against an increasingly wishy-washy and hyper-moralistic president. After the Soviet invasion of Afghanistan and the taking of U.S. hostages in Teheran, a roller-coaster effect was in order, but there can be no question that the roller-coaster had already begun its ride before external events propelled it along. The late 1970s were a period of reexamination in American life, when economic difficulties and global complexities urged a return to basic and fundamental cliches about the good old days. No president, and certainly not one as weak as Jimmy Carter, could have avoided being swept along by the frenzy of concern over national weakness that characterized the United States as the 1980s began.

If the Carter presidency is an exception to the generalization that a relationship exists between presidential power and negative perceptions of the Soviet threat, the Reagan Administration confirms the trend many times over. Ronald Reagan and his advisors came to power with a prepared agenda carefully worked out in advance. They were going to repeal the Great Society and as much of the New Deal as they could. They were going to try and obtain strategic superiority over the Soviet Union. They were going to redistribute income from the poor and middle class to the rich. Ironically, though the goals of the Reagan Administration were conservative, the means were liberal, for it required unusual presidential power—hitherto a strong tenet of liberal faith—to make changes as dramatic as these. Since the welfare state was created through strong executive leadership, it could only be dismantled likewise. Ronald Reagan needed all the power he could accumulate if he were to have a chance to roll back governmental power.

Even though the third peak of anti-Soviet sentiment in the postwar period was Congressionally inspired, it fit well with the plans of the incoming Reagan Administration. One of the most important of Reagan's electoral victories in his first year, for example, was to win a procedural point by which Congress voted on his budget as a whole, not piece by piece. This enabled the Administration to provide executive leadership missing since the days before Watergate. Just as Reagan borrowed significant policies from the Kennedy Administration, like general tax cuts and military spending, he borrowed as well Kennedy's sense of a stage-managed, highly orchestrated presidency responding to world events. Once the Administration suffered the embarrassment of having the president asleep while fighter planes were engaged in combat over Libya, his advisors made it a point to appear to be constantly "on top of" world events. Thus the Reagan Adminstration, like previous Democratic Administrations, used the language of presidential prerogatives to argue for its point of view. When a resolution in the House calling for a nuclear freeze came within two votes of passage, the Reagan Administration opposed it, not on grounds of content, but with the argument that it would tie the president's hands in negotiating with the Russians, a page lifted out of Kennedy's book. Democratic concern with presidential power and the Soviet threat were once again linked, except that the Republicans had come to embody conceptions of a strong executive in the face of an internally divided Democratic Party.

So long as the Reagan Administration successfully manages to raise the spectre of the Soviet threat at opportune moments, the Congress will continue to sacrifice its already waning powers. Rapid turnover in Congress, the weakening of the political parties and enormous public distrust and unhappiness with the legislative branch have combined to push Congress to an increasingly ceremonial role. For Congress to avoid this fate, it will have to take budgetary matters into it own hands, which means standing up and resisting exaggerated claims from the executive branch about the immediacy of the Soviet threat.

A Carter Advisor Speaks on Presidential Power

...it is essential that there be more effective centralized control over East-West economic relations within the executive branch of government. This is necessary so that the various decisions that have to be made concerning trade, technological transfers, scientific contacts, credits, and grain exports will be brought together at a single point and effectively related to the foreign policy purposes that the United States is pursuing at any given time. This can only be done adequately through the framework of the National Security Council (NSC)...

The central need is to provide the president with the means to engage in creative and flexible economic diplomacy with the Soviets. There has been much discussion recently about untying the president's hands in foreign policy...It is equally important to untie the president's hands so that the United States can capitalize on its economic resources in its relations with the Soviets...

It is fairly clear that the nature of the Soviet political system prevents the Soviets from correcting their economic deficiencies. It would be truly ironic, even tragic, if it should turn out that the nature of the American political system prevents this nation from capitalizing on its very real economic advantages. That need not be the case.

Samuel P. Huntington, then coordinator of national security planning at the National Security Council, speaking at West Point, June 1978.

Huntington, who gained enormous notoriety when he wrote a report for the Trilateral Commission arguing that America had become too democratic, here urges centralization of policy in a manner that has become almost reflexive for believers in strong presidential action.

Unless one wishes to claim that the relationship between attacks on presidential power and the cultivation of the Soviet· threat is purely coincidental, the following relationships seem worth pondering:

1. An important reason for the cycle of anti-Soviet perceptions may lie in the fact that strong executive leadership is necessary to govern an advanced capitalist society with a global foreign policy, while ideology, tradition, and culture in America all conspire against the permanent existence of a strong presidency. In this sense, one factor associated with the frequency of the Soviet threat is the weakness of the executive branch, for if its power were more secure, it would not need to exaggerate external measures in order to hold on to the power that it had accumulated. Truman, Kennedy and Carter were all in precarious political positions when the Soviet threat increased.

2. Negative perceptions of Soviet intentions are likely to arise at times when an activist-oriented president has just been elected. If the new president faces a "natural" cycle in which power is due to pass away from the presidency, he will find that anti-Soviet feelings generate an atmosphere which preserves presidential power. Increasingly, each new administration seeks to distance itself from the previous one by proving its "genuine" anti-Soviet intentions.

3. Thus, domestic political struggles over the nature of the presidency have some relationship to, even if they do not necessarily cause, peaks in the perception of anti-Soviet hostility. A study by the Brookings Institution, for example, found that the number of foreign adventures rose as the popularity of the president went up.[54] The best method of generating broad support in a pluralistic and highly fractured political system seems to be through foreign policy actions.

4. While at one time the Democrats were the party that linked the Soviet threat with an expansion of presidential power, the Reagan experience indicates that the relationship is bipartisan. Legislative responsibility over both fiscal affairs and social policy will be difficult to achieve in an age of austerity unless Congress reasserts its control over the defense budget, which it could do only by meeting head on, and dismissing, the exaggerated claims of a Soviet threat that emanate so frequently from the White House.

CHAPTER V

THE POLITICS OF
INTER-SERVICE RIVALRIES

The modern executive is not only one branch of government among many, but a system of government unto itself containing numerous branches within it. As the presidency has become more vital to the governing of modern economy with a global foreign policy, the most important political conflicts begin to take place, not over it, but within it. For example, disputes between the CIA and the National Security Council often become bitter, as do arguments between the NSC and the Department of State. Those debates in turn lead to changes in American foreign policy.

Even within single branches of the executive, disputes over "turf" are likely to be serious. In this chapter, I will argue that the most important of these disputes—arguments between the military services for a greater share of the defense dollar—are directly related to the peaks of anti-Soviet perception. My point will be that the most negative perceptions of an external enemy tend to occur when the military services cannot agree on their proper share of the budget and make their differences public, whereas the valleys in anti-Soviet perception occur at times of relative peace between the three service branches.

In an age of nuclear weapons and multifaceted wars, the distinction between an army (land), and navy (sea), and an air force (air) makes less sense than it ever did, militarily speaking. From a strictly geo-political point of view, the nature of modern war demands an integrated fighting organization, one that can combine land, air, and sea operations. But however much sense integration makes militarily, there are substantial obstacles to such unification. Each military service is a bureaucratic empire, jealously guarding its self-interest by exaggerating what it does best and denigrating the capabilities of its opponents. Each, moreover, has its own constituency—contractors, legislators, supportive interest groups and ideologues—that it can mobilize at a moment's notice when it feels that it is about to be short-changed. Sometimes the wars fought between the service branches seem to rival the wars fought overseas in their intensity.

Since the end of World War II there have been repeated attempts to establish or to disestablish the equilibrium in power between the services. Such attempts generally occur in one of two ways. First, one branch, convinced that it has gained power over the others, attempts to sponsor a "reorganization" that will solidify into bureaucratic permanence its hegemony. Alternatively, another branch, feeling that it is losing power, will attempt some kind of scheme so that it can recoup its losses. In either case, whenever such a struggle takes place, it will be in the interest of somebody to exaggerate negative perceptions of an external enemy, either to hold on to what they have or to expand the scope of their holdings. In this way, the Soviet threat has achieved a position of prominence in American life whenever the equilibrium among the military branches is upset.

Until the advent of the Reagan Administration, the sharpest example of the relationship between military infighting and the exaggeration of anti-Soviet perceptions took place as the Cold War began. World War II had made it clear that there would have to be some unification of the armed services, since the practice of giving each substantial autonomy tended to interfere with effective war planning. At the same time, all the traditional bureaucratic devices that prevent rational integration were sure to be pulled out if anyone seriously tried to bring a sense of order and planning to the fighting of wars. Caught between the military need for integration and the political realities that prevented it, policymakers sought a compromise. The National Security Act of 1947 gave them one. While unifying the services under a Secretary of Defense (and providing for a Joint Chiefs of Staff), it also allowed each its own relative autonomy within the new structure. All that was accomplished, in other words, was to transfer the struggles from ones that took place between positions in the cabinet to ones that took place within one super-agency.[55]

These battles were exacerbated by the constituency politics that had developed over each service branch. The Navy Department, for example, tended to have its support among patrician families along the East Coast who, whether Republican or Democratic in sympathy, leaned toward strong leadership and the kind of active presidency symbolized by the Roosevelts (both former Secretaries of the Navy). James Forrestal, the first Secretary of Defense, was very much in this tradition. The Army, in contrast, was rooted in the South. Its politics tended to be Democratic (as befitted a Southern institution). Moreover, because of the Army was the most labor-intensive service, housing huge numbers of men from working class and poor backgrounds, it generally took an outlook on the world that was not ultra-reactionary. Army men often supported the welfare state and believed in the kind of active government that had characterized the U.S. since the New Deal.[56] Finally, the strength of the Air Force lay in the Far West, where exceptionally conservative politics and isolationism were strong. Most Air Force leaders were Republicans, tied to defense contractors that wanted to arm in a kind of Fortress America style, relying on huge, capital-intensive systems that carried with them enormous profits.

Both Franklin Roosevelt and Harry Truman had followed policies that tended to benefit the Army and the Navy at the expense of the Air Corps. But the Air Corps was convinced that the future belonged to airpower, for in the postwar period nuclear weapons were the number one reality, and it semed as if the logical way to deliver such weapons was on airplanes. In addition, the burgeoning conservative sentiment and desire for normality that was a feature of the 1948-50 period worked to the advantage of the Air Corps, for it could offer the maximum protection at the least cost, fiscal and psychological. For all these reasons, the Air Corps began a campaign the moment the war ended to divorce itself from the Army and then to expand itself relative to its rivals. A commission headed by Thomas Finletter produced a report called *Survival in the Air Age* that trumpeted the virtues of a new service.[57] Support among scientists and intellectuals was won by the creation of the RAND corporation in California that was tied to the new service. Once created, the Air Force seemed determined to take control over the military establishment.

In their campaign for hegemony, prominent Air Force officials found themselves distorting the Soviet threat, for they needed a credible external enemy as a rationale for their campaign. Air Force

General Carl Spaatz, who led the fight for his service, blithely stated the case as follows: "The low grade terror of Russia which paralyzes Italy, France, England, and Scandinavia can be kept from our own country by an ability on our part to deliver atomic destruction by air. If Russia does strike the U.S., *as she will if her present frame of mind continues*, only a powerful air force in being can strike back fast enough, and hard enough to prevent the utter destruction of our nation."[58] (Emphasis added). When a war scare broke out over Czechoslovakia in the spring of 1948, the Air Force saw its chance. Air Force Secretary Stuart Symington (one of the Democrats who had associated himself with the new service) created something called the 70-Group to lobby for greater funds for his service. He was successful. The military budget was entirely rewritten for FY 1949, and the share going to the Air Force had doubled. It had become clear to all how fanning the flames of an overseas crisis could be used to protect (and even expand) bureaucratic turf at home.

One important question remained unanswered: would the increase given to the Air Force be at the expense of the other services? So long as the defense budget was held constant—which Truman was determined to do—then the obvious answer was yes. In this case, the other services had to find some way to protect their empires. One way was to highlight Soviet strength in a particular area, as the Navy had done the previous year when it argued that the Russian submarine fleet was stronger than Hitler's had been. But when the Navy lost its campaign for a flush-deck carrier in 1949,[59] it began to emphasize the overall threat from the Soviet Union rather than the specific threat posed by particular weapons. In that way, there would be enormous pressure on Truman to raise the ceiling that he had imposed on the military budget as a whole. With the ceiling lifted, the Air Force's gains would not be taken out of the hides of the other services.

The Air Force had shown how one service branch, trying to solidify its hegemony over the others, could use an exaggeration of the Soviet threat to achieve its purposes. By the late 1950s, as the second peak of anti-Soviet belligerency was building up, the Army began to show how a branch that was losing power could also use the Soviet threat in order to regain its prestige. Strengthened by vastly increased budgets, the Air Force had become more complacent during the 1950s, convinced that the discovery of nuclear weapons had made the other services obsolete. Although Eisenhower had been an Army man, he went along with this point of view, for his fiscal conservatism pushed him to support the Air

Force's claim of a "bigger bang for the buck." So sure was the Air Force of its superiority that it failed to notice a rising challenge from a new generation of Army officers.

A cosmopolitan Army Chief of Staff named Maxwell Taylor launched a campaign during the closing years of the Eisenhower era to return the Army to its former position of prominence. Taylor was convinced of two things. First, though nuclear weapons were impressive, they were not likely to be used in the kind of "brushfire" wars the U.S. was likely to be fighting. Second, relying on them meant that the U.S. was becoming weaker, not stronger, for it was putting its military eggs in the wrong basket. Based upon these points, Taylor, in various Department of Defense internal memoranda and in his popular book *The Uncertain Trumpet*, urged the U.S. to build more conventional arms.[60] In addition, since any conflicts in Europe were likely to involve nuclear weapons (the stakes were that high), he urged that the U.S. think about areas of the world outside Europe, and especially about the Third World.

The only problem with Taylor's conception was that it was unclear how the interests of the United States were intertwined with the peripheral countries of the world. Latin America had always been a direct source of interest, but what role should the U.S. take toward countries in Asia, Africa and the Middle East? Eisenhower, and the Joint Chiefs, had specifically rejected an intervention into Vietnam in 1954 on the grounds that it was not worth the cost. To make it appear as if these countries were of vital and direct concern, Taylor and like-minded people claimed that the *real* enemy in such circumstances was the Russians. From this point of view, any revolution in the Third World was automatically a victory for the U.S.S.R. since it diminished the power and prestige of the United States.

Ironically, Taylor's view of the world gave the Russians more credit than they deserved. In the real world, the Russians were ambivalent toward the instability in the Third World and did not know what to make of all these nationalistic rebellions. But Taylor and other cold war enthusiasts like Walt Rostow, by seeing Russians everywhere, created a self-fulfilling prophecy. Since in their view the Russians *had* to be involved, then for all intents and purposes, the U.S. acted as if they were, whether they were or not. Direct U.S. intervention in the Third World would have to increase, as would the role of the Army, the most appropriate service for counter-insurgency warfare.

Kennedy, as a Democrat, leaned toward the Army view of events. He made Taylor a major figure in his administration. He increased the budget of the Army. He sponsored the notion of counter-insurgency warfare around which the Army was staging its comeback. In short, domestic political considerations—especially the link between the Army and the Democratic Party—had much to do with the attractiveness of a new strategic theory in the early 1960s. Since no new theory could be implemented without a revised (and revived) version of the Soviet threat, the Soviet threat was duly revised (and revived). From now on, the Russians were seen as wanting to expand into the Third World in exactly the same way an earlier generation viewed them as anxious to get their hands on France and Germany.

Kennedy also talked a great deal about bringing the Department of Defense under control. Under Robert McNamara's secretaryship, cost accountants, engineers, and systems analysts took over the Pentagon budget and announced that only cost-effective programs would be approved. Had this actually taken place, the military men would have been at each other's throats. In actuality, McNamara greatly expanded the overall military budget, and relative peace was brought to the war among the service branches. As the budgets rose during the 1960s, perceptions of the Soviet threat began to subside, even though the U.S. was fighting in a war. With plenty of money to spend, no military service needed to sound the tocsin to obtain more.

The costs of bringing peace to Washington's inter-service rivalry were enormously high, as all participants realized. Furnishing each service with its own pet projects brought about the reality feared by conservatives since 1946: deficit spending, high taxes, and uncontrollable inflation. Indeed by the time Nixon was elected, the economy seemed almost completely out of control, and at least one prominent reason for its erratic behavior was the drain that defense spending, especially but not exclusively in Vietnam, had upon domestic economic performance. Vietnam also diverted funds from Soviet-oriented services like the Strategic Air Command, leading them to revive the spectre of the Soviet threat in order to make a come-back.

How to Combat Inter-Service Rivalry

"The greater our variety of weapons, the more political choices we can make in any given situation."

John F. Kennedy (1961)

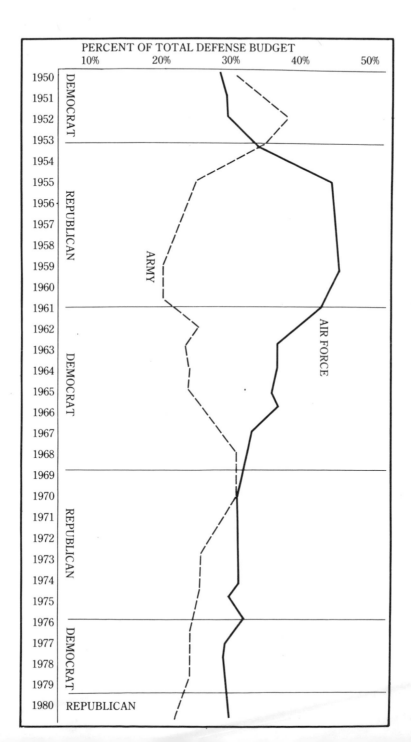

Nixon began to realize that some attempt to make choices in national defense would have to be made. Although military men think of themselves as apolitical creatures, interested not in partisanship but only in the national defense, the pattern since 1950 shows that the Army tends to fare better under Democrats and the Air Force under Republicans. As the above chart reveals, the Air Force budget increased (and the Army budget decreased) after 1953 when Eisenhower became president; this pattern was reversed again under Kennedy and Johnson; and it reversed again under Nixon and Ford. (During the Carter years there was a decrease, as we would expect, in the Air Force's share of the budget, but there was no appreciable increase in the Army's share; the Navy, Carter's own service, did relatively well, but the largest categories of expenditure increase under Carter were non-service related ones like military aid to other countries).

Strategic theory often follows the budget, not the other way around. As the importance of the Air Force under Nixon began to increase, for example, Maxwell Taylor's emphasis on guerilla wars was played down in favor of a direct counting of strategic weapons between the Soviet Union and the United States. Nixon's Secretaries of Defense repudiated McNamara's notion of Mutually Assured Destruction in favor of doctrines that emphasized the ability of the United States to destroy Soviet life. These new doctrines were far more compatible with the Air Force's outlook on the world than they were with the Army's.

By the time of the Carter presidency, economic constraints were working against *all* the military services, indeed against every activity undertaken by government. Carter's inclination was to favor the Army, but fiscal realities prevented him from doing so. Unlike Nixon and Ford, Carter cancelled deployment of the B-1 bomber, although Congress kept alive the possibility of its revival. Moreover, both in PRM-10 and in his budget messages, Carter gave a more prominent role to conventional weapons, which remained the preserve of the Army and the Navy. (Indeed, the ill-fated SALT II treaty, by limiting strategic weapons generally built by the Air Force would, if passed, have enabled the Administration to expand even more its conventional arms.) By identifying the Middle East as a crucial problem area, Carter relied on lightening-quick deployment of tanks and helicopters, not massive nuclear weapons delivered from planes that fly in the stratosphere. Not surprisingly, the Army and Navy were encouraged by these developments, while Air Force officials murmured dark hints about deteriorating national resolve.

During the Carter years allegations of the Soviet threat began once more to build up, and, expectedly, the Air Force took the lead in the new crusade. There were representatives of the other services involved, such as Admiral Elmo Zumwalt, an early exponent of the present danger, but he was outdone in patriotic zeal by disgruntled Air Force generals. Loss of the B-1 was a bitter blow to the Air Force, which in any case had seen the increased obsolescence of manned strategic bombers, upon which it had once rested its future. By developing pieces of the cruise missile, the MX, and airlift support for quick-strike conventional wars, the Air Force had done rather well for itself, even under Carter, but feelings of deprivation on these matters are always relative, not absolute. By concentrating on the systems it lost, the Air Force complained that America's entire defense was in a shambles, leading it to play a major role in the militaristic atmosphere of the late 1970s. One of the leading proponents of the Team B report, the first systematic document in the most recent revival of the Soviet threat, was retired Air Force General Keegan. Leading a one-man crusade against the Carter military budgets, Keegan eventually rallied all those forces in the Washington bureaucratic wars who felt victimized by the changes in military strategy demanded by the economic austerity of the late 1970s. The third peak in anti-Soviet hostility originated in the Air Force's sense of relative deprivation during the Carter years, though all three services experienced frustration and anger.

Once the Reagan Administration took office, predictable statements about the Soviet lead in air force technology became familiar on Capitol Hill. "As a result of the steady expansion and modernization of Soviet strategic forces," commented Air Force Chief of Staff General Lew Allen Jr., "there has been a dramatic shift in the strategic balance. The momentum of Soviet programs has begun to tilt the equation significantly in Moscow's favor."[61] Statements like this have become somewhat routine when a new administration takes office. What was less routine was the attempt by the Reagan Administration to expand the Air Force budget beyond all expectations. For fiscal 1983, for example, Reagan asked Congress to approve the following: $4.8 billion for a new version of the B-1 bomber, which many critics charged would be obsolete the moment it was built; $4.46 billion for the MX, up from $1.97 billion for fiscal 1982; $860 million for two models of the C-5 cargo plane; $882 million for air launched cruise missiles; and a build-up of Air Force personnel from 580,000 to 640,000 over five years. The totals represented a 12.2% "real" increase in the share of the military budget claimed by the Air Force.[62] One staff member for a Congressional committee told the *New York Times*: "They've had all these 'wish lists' in their desk drawers for years and now, for the first time in years, you have an administration that wants to spend money on defense and these guys are just whipping out the lists and saying. 'Here, here, it's urgent.' "[63] Never before had one service branch obtained so much from one budget.

Have the Russians made such gains in their own air force as to justify these expenditures? Skepticism may be appropriate given the distribution of the Reagan largesse. It is recognized by many military specialists that the surest way to strengthen one's defenses is to keep already existing systems working satisfactorily. Yet as the accompanying chart shows, those items in the Air Force budget slated to rise the most are "big ticket" projects like new procurement and military construction, especially when compared to operations and personnel. The shape of the Air Force budget— huge increases devoted to the most expensive items—suggests more a political grab-bag than a well thought out and carefully considered response to a foreign threat. Rather than the Soviet threat coming first and the budget as its reponse, the Reagan years represent an attempt to raise the budget first and develop the threat as a response to that.

Growth in the Air Force Budget

Rounded figures in each category, in millions of dollars. Data for each fiscal year are from the President's 1983 budget report and do not include pay raises that will be submitted soon to Congress. Calculations for real growth take into account these raises. Fiscal year 1983 forecasts are based on an inflation rate of 7.6%

	1982	1983	real growth
Research, development, training and education	$8,876	$11,220	$19.2%
Aircraft procurement	14,022	17,757	17.9
Missile procurement	4,574	6,828	39.1
Other procurement	5,407	5,845	2.2
Military construction	1,772	2,224	19.3
Military personnel	11,055	12,927	2.6
Operation, maintenance	18,442	20,473	5.5
Stock fund	79	162	92.8
Family housing	737	938	19.9
TOTAL	**$64,964**	**$78,373**	**12.2%***

*Excludes military family housing   *Source: U.S. Air Force*

During previous periods of anti-Soviet concern, rivalry between the three service branches, as I have tried to show in this chapter, were responsible for the tendency to increase the rhetoric about external threats in order to prevent losses in bureaucratic skirmishes. During the Reagan years, these trends continued, but with an added irony. The Air Force itself in recent years has split into factions of its own: a tactical air force, often identified with the service as a whole; a strategic air force composed of B-52 officers; and a missile command in charge of the silo-based nuclear weapons. Now these factions compete among themselves the way the service branches used to compete with each other. When a new weapon like the B-1 bomber is proposed, the debates *within* the Air Force rival in their intensity the debates that once took place between the Air Force and the Army. Such bureaucratic politics do not make for rational and subdued calculations of enemy capabilities and intentions when the number of players who have a vested interest in exaggerating external threats increases so sharply.

The Navy's Plan Over Five Years

Schedules for shipbuilding, conversions, recalls and major overhaul of ships, and for procurement of aircraft. Figures in 1983 dollars, not adjusted for inflation.

SHIPS

1983	25 ships	$18.7 billion
1984	23 ships	12.5 billion
1985	29 ships	16.8 billion
1986	33 ships	20.1 billion
1987	39 ships	28.1 billion
total	**149 ships**	**96.2 billion**

AIRCRAFT

1983	288 planes	$11.6 billion
1984	359 planes	12.9 billion
1985	397 planes	15.6 billion
1986	431 planes	15.8 billion
1987	442 planes	15.8 billion
total	**1,917 planes**	**71.7 billion**

Source: Department of the Navy

Not content with these increases in the Air Force budget, the Reagan Administration has also been sympathetic to complaints from the Navy that it has been shortchanged in recent years. Reagan's Secretary of the Navy, John Lehman, is known as an extreme hawk on military matters, but unlike some of his colleagues, Lehman has come right out and said that his goal is to win strategic superiority over the Russians: "Clear maritime superiority must be required. This is not a debatable strategy. It is a national objective, a security imperative."[64] Lehman is not one to stint on his requests, planning, as he is, a Navy that would contain 600 ships and 1900 aircraft.

Behind the figures and requests lies a revised strategy for the seas. Convinced that in the future resource wars between the U.S. and other societies, including perhaps even current allies, will be on the agenda, the Reagan Administration is attempting to create a global presence that would be effective, mobile, and capable of sustained action. While the rhetoric to justify the increases in the Navy budget are based on the usual incantation of the Soviet threat, the plans of the Reagan Administration are far more offensive than defensive, envisioning a strengthened America that, as in the days of Teddy Roosevelt, can throw its weight around by sending its ships wherever needed.

To summarize, the following relationships seem worth emphasizing:

1. Anti-Soviet perceptions will tend to rise when there is no rough balance between the military services in terms of their relative shares of the budget and one or another service seeks to enhance its relative position as a result.

2. Equilibria tend to break down when a new political party enters the White House. Traditionally, Democrats favor the Army, while Republicans incline toward the Air Force. (The Navy has advocates in both parties but, historically, has been associated with the "moderate" wing of the Republican Party, now almost obliterated.).

3. The most time-honored way of reestablishing an equilibrium among the service branches is to expand the overall military budget. Thus a recurrent pattern emerges: a new party comes to power; that party then shifts money toward its favorite service; those branches that stand to lose will "discover" the Soviet threat and issue harrowing warnings about America's future; at this point, presidents back off from confrontation (not wanting to appear weak in the face of an external threat); as they back off, the budget begins to climb, a new equilibrium is established, and the

most negative perceptions of the Soviet Union begin to taper off. Ronald Reagan has attempted to settle inter-service rivalries through a deluge of defense "goodies."

4. During the Reagan years, the pattern of interservice rivalry, disturbing as it has become, has been complemented by a tendency for each of the services to divide into factions which use the Soviet threat against each other. The result is that the size and scope of the military budget seems to have as much to do with bureaucratic politics as with national security. A society committed to the pursuit of self-interest finds it difficult to protect itself in a rational way when to do so means to cooperate, rather than compete, over the nature of the external threats to it.

CHAPTER VI

FOREIGN POLICY COALITIONS
AND THE SOVIET THREAT

To this point, my explanation for the peaks in anti-Soviet perceptions has concentrated exclusively on domestic politics, as if events taking place in the rest of the world were irrelevant. Those events must be included in any such analysis, as I will begin to do in this chapter. But, interestingly enough, many of the debates over foreign policy that influence perceptions of the U.S.S.R. have little to do with Russia directly. Instead, anti-Soviet perceptions often become a tactic for winning support for attempts to reorient foreign policy toward totally different parts of the world.

In a democratic society like the United States, foreign policy cannot simply be made directly by a small elite unconcerned about interest groups or public opinion. It is neccessary to build a coalition of interests around a specific foreign policy, and to win public support for that policy through mass appeals. Such tasks are not easy, for highly divergent economic, ideological, and partisan disagreements exist about what the main locus of U.S. foreign policy should be. In this chapter I will argue that negative perceptions of Soviet conduct are an important device by which certain kinds of foreign policy coalitions try to win support for a change in the locus of U.S. foreign policy. More specifically, I will argue that the first peak in anti-Soviet hostility was related to an attempt by a European-oriented elite to shift policy away from a pro-Asian direction; that the second peak involved an attempt by foreign policy activists concerned with the Third World to reorient policy in that direction; and that the third peak has much to do with attempts to form a new foreign policy coalition in the wake of America's defeat in Vietnam. In short, the underlying point of this chapter is that foreign policy is relevant to understanding the rise and fall of the Soviet threat but it is not always foreign policy toward Russia; negative perceptions of Soviet conduct become *instrumental* tactics, designed to achieve other ends.

One of the most important disagreements within the foreign policy establishment until the late 1940s was between Europhiles, who thought of Europe as the quintessence of Western Civilization, and Asia-firsters, who were concerned about bringing "civilization" to the East. Asia-firsters tended to be tied to businessmen interested in expanding into new markets and territories.[65] They possessed an outlook on the world, and a location in the structure of production, that was quite different from those oriented toward Europe. Generally associated with new and more competitive industries located in the West, they were conservative in their politics, and were suspicious of the use of big government for any purpose other than protecting U.S. businesses through tariffs. When they thought of overseas expansion, they envisioned business being free to move anywhere around the globe in search for markets. Since European markets had been tied up for centuries, they generally viewed the Third World avariciously, and typically had a special interest in Asia, where more potential consumers exist than anywhere else. If they had had their way, American foreign policy would have been characterized by substantial help for business expansion; low military budgets except when absolutely necessary; a reluctance to endorse foreign aid; and a suspicion of permanent treaties, covert action, and other ways by which the U.S. could become entrapped in the internal wranglings of other countries, especially European ones.

European-oriented policymakers viewed the Asia-firsters roughly the way box holders at the opera think of wrestling fans. Generally men of considerable hereditary wealth, long since removed from the nitty-gritty of making money, the Europhiles were concerned with long-term global stability, not immediate profit. With ties to both the financial world and the monopoly sector—and with a domestic ideology that stressed long-term reform in the interests of preserving the system as a whole—these men were far more sympathetic to using the power of government to organize the world than their Asian inclined colleagues. They thought of the world in terms of nation states, not specific business firms, and they wanted to see the American state be the unsurpassed power in the world. This meant a tolerance for high defense budgets, a standing army, support for foreign aid and covert intelligence, and a positive penchant for becoming involved in the affairs of other countries. To them, the ideal world would be one in which all Americans willingly shouldered the responsibilities of global leadership and permitted class-conscious State Department planners to seek peace through balance-of-power policies.[66]

Underlying the debate between the Asia-firsters and the Euro-capitalists were differences in economics that made the issues so bitter. The Europhiles tended to be free traders. In their view, capital should be free to move around wherever it can be cost efficient, regardless of national boundaries. But they also understood that no system of free trade and currency convertability could work unless one state were powerful enough to enforce it, as Britain had been able to do in the nineteenth century. The pro-European vision asked for domestic sacrifice in the name of long term patterns of growth in the world economy. Inefficient American industries would have to fold if they could not compete in world markets. Jobs at home might have to be sacrificed to protect capital mobility. The U.S. would have to accept balance of payment problems if they were necessary to rebuild Europe. In short, the economic program of the large corporations and financial interests. that supported the Europe-firsters called for a denial of immediate gratification, not only on the part of labor, but also on the part of competitive-sector business. It was a program that, by itself, could never have attracted much mass appeal, especially in a country like the United States that had a long protectionist history.

Opposition to the free trade principles of the European-oriented elite came, not unexpectedly, from nationalistic business-people who needed protection to compete in world markets, from labor unions that wanted to protect their members' jobs, and from all those people who, for whatever reason, did not want their tax dollars propping up other governments around the world. Economic nationalism, in addition, had far more popular appeal than free trade liberalism. It did not ask for sacrifices. It put the needs of Americans first. It spoke of an identity of interests between capitalists and workers in keeping business at home. (In the 1980s, when American factories are moving to Hong Kong and Mexico, the old Asia-first bloc has become an advocate of free trade.) It was, in short, the more "democratic" alternative in the sense that its popularity was, from the beginning, inherently greater.

Throughout most of the twentieth century, the Asia-first mentality had had substantial influence on American policy, from the acquisition of the Philippines in 1898 to the furor over the "loss" of China in the 1950s. Even as Hitler invaded country after country in the late 1930s, the strong and unbreakable Asia-first mentality prevented Franklin Roosevelt from intervening on the side of the European democracies. It was not until an Asian power, Japan, bombed an installation in the Far West, Pearl Harbor, that enough consensus existed in the United States to support the war effort. When World War II began, in other words, the Asia-first mentality was still in a superior position to the Europeanists.

A significant number of State Department officials hoped that the coming of World War II would prevent the U.S. from ever again returning to its anti-European proclivities. As the war came to an end, they were determined to find a way to preserve their emphasis on Europe (and the Mediterranean) as the center of both world civilization and of American concern abroad.

Numerous problems stood in the path of the Eurocapitalists in 1945. For one thing, the Asia-first sentiment, held in check during the war, was bound to explode once Germany and Japan had been defeated. Part of the right-wing counterattack after the war would surely involve the direction of U.S. foreign policy. In addition, the key to a stable Europe was Germany, yet the U.S. had just fought a major war against the Germans. In order for the Europeanists to have their way, Germany would have to be transformed from enemy to friend, and in the quickest possible time.

Beyond these problems, conditions in Europe were rather depressing to the Europeanists. The war-devastated economies of the continent would be unable to recover without American help. Yet there was not much sympathy in America for providing that assistance. Many people in Congress felt that if Europe was unable to defend itself, the U.S. should stay out of its affairs. Massive aid programs would only entangle the United States in situations that it could not control and lead the country, once again, into war.

In the late 1940s, negative images of Soviet expansionism became the device by which free trade liberals were able to overcome the inherently elitist aspects of their program and to sell it as having general appeal. By combining the free trade vision with the Soviet threat, the Europhiles were able to characterize protectionists and Asia-firsters as short-sighted, selfish, and uncharitable in the face of the world's problems. They were also accused of being stingy on matters of national defense and of encouraging war and aggression. So long as the debate was posed in this fashion, the European-oriented free traders could dominate it, something they would never have been able to do without the Soviet threat. Thus the Russians were used to make a free trade program acceptable in a democratic society.

The first test of the political clout of the two foreign policy factions came in 1946 as the U.S. Congress considered a massive loan to the British. Conservative opposition, led by Ohio Senator Robert Taft, was fierce. Congressional leaders told Truman that the only way to pass the bill was to make a strongly anti-Soviet speech claiming that Britain's future was in danger from the Russians. Truman said no. Congressional leaders made the claim in any case, and the loan passed. Within two years, Truman would no longer be so reticent.[67]

The British loan, as conservatives correctly charged, was a foot-in-the-door for more elaborate aid proposals. European-oriented policymakers had in mind an audacious plan to reconstruct the entire economy of Western Europe with an aid program so vast that capital flows around the world would be permanently altered. When the idea was unveiled at Harvard University by Secretary of State George Marshall, the opposition mobilized. Passage of the Marshall Plan, most policymakers realized, would so commit the U.S. to the future of a capitalist Europe that there would be no turning back.

The Marshall Plan was, in the end, approved by Congress. But Truman had been forced to pay a price. No longer could he refuse, as he had done with the British loan, to arouse the spectre of the Soviet threat. Like the Air Force, Truman opted to manipulate domestic perceptions of the crisis in Czechoslovakia in February 1948 in order to build support for his program. Speaking in dramatic terms, the Truman Administration charged that a freedom-loving country had been invaded by totalitarianism for the second time in a decade. Even though U.S. officials had concluded that Czechoslovakia had already been a communist state before February 1948, (they had refused on that ground to give it foreign aid, for example, thereby insuring greater popularity for the Russians in that country) the solidification of Russian control became instrumental in reshaping domestic politics within the United States. The Marshall Plan was passed after Truman delivered a war scare speech in March.

This was no one-time-only piece of legislation. For the Marshall Plan to be effective in rebuilding European capitalism, a long term commitment to aid was necessary. For this reason, passage of the Marshall Plan did not quell the rhetoric of the Soviet threat but institutionalized it. Now there would have to be proof every year of the evil designs of the Kremlin (and the efficacy of foreign aid in stymying those designs) before renewal monies would be forthcoming. As Europe began its economic miracle, some of the more extreme rhetoric did relax, but further innovations in U.S.-Europe relations—particularly the NATO treaty and support for European integration—required the cultivation of negative images of Soviet intentions in order to pass through a Congress that still looked longingly on the Far East and suspiciously at Europe.[68]

These events show that the first peak in anti-Soviet hostility did have a foreign policy dimension, but one that was not exclusively concerned with the Soviet Union. To be sure, Russia was part of Europe and American policymakers were genuinely concerned about the threat posed by the Soviet Union to our European allies. But at the same time, a significant number of policymakers were more directly interested in building up the economic might of Europe, especially Germany, and the fear of the Soviets was to them an instrument to achieve this alternative objective. The events surrounding the Marshall Plan and the development of a free trade economy are an excellent illustration of how anti-Soviet perceptions became essential to foreign policy objectives that are tangential to a *direct* concern with the Soviet Union.

Events taking place in the real world are also related to the second peak of anti-Soviet hostility, although once again they involve U.S.-Soviet relations only tangentially. The activists that came to power with Kennedy were concerned with changing Eisenhower's priorities in two ways. First, while they were satisfied that a pro-European inclination had been adopted, they were concerned that it was not strong enough. Second, and more important, they wanted to shift American policy to a greater confrontation with revolutions taking place in the Third World. Exaggerating the danger posed by the Russians became instrumental to both of these purposes.

During the 1950s, the Asia-firsters made an attempted comeback under Senator Joseph McCarthy, who tried to purge the State Department of its European orientation and led an attack on the China experts who, to him, were not sufficiently enraptured by the anti-communists in that part of the world. As a result, the pro-European policies adopted in the late 1940s were in danger. In addition, some Europeans, like DeGaulle, were showing disturbing signs of independence, and the economic costs of the pro-Europe alliance were high, as measured by balance of payments deficits that started to increase during the 1950s.

The sense of urgency about Europe that captivated Kennedy's advisors was reinforced by their perception that under Eisenhower the alliance had begun to atrophy. In the view of the Kennedy men,

Eisenhower had made needless concessions to the Soviets in 1959 over Berlin and was going to make more at the 1960 summit. This, they argued, was weakening American resolve, and, as a first order of business, the new administration should put the Russians on notice that the U.S. would not back down on its commitment to West Berlin. In March and May of 1961, Kennedy made bold speeches promising greater U.S. rearmament, directed principally against the Russians. His advisor, Dean Acheson, called for an explicit confrontation with the Russians over Berlin, and Kennedy was willing to listen.[69] Facing all this, Khrushchev upped the ante and threatened to sign a separate peace treaty with East Germany. The stage was set for a confrontation over Europe, a situation that Eisenhower had tried to avoid. Kennedy went to Berlin and announced that he was a Berliner. The Soviets put up a wall, a concrete symbol of the bankruptcy of their own policies.[70] One effect of all these moves was to restore a European consciousness to American affairs. More military aid went to NATO, troop commitments to Germany increased, and the military alliance between the U.S. and Western Europe was solidified.

But equally as important to the Kennedy Administration as the firming up of the European alliance was its concern with the Third World. In Asia and Africa, newly independent countries were coming into existence every year. Populous, strategically important, and loaded with raw materials, these countries were clearly going to play a major role in future international politics. The West's policy toward the Third World had until then been a colonial one, which did not make much sense for the last half of the twentieth century. The Kennedy Administration took the lead in trying to fashion a policy that would be more appropriate to this new reality than the simple business-dominated neo-colonialism of the Eisenhower Administration.

Kennedy's thinking on the Third World was heavily influenced by a group of intellectuals in Cambridge, Massachusetts who had been studying the revolutionary movements in those countries. These men—Walt Rostow, Lincoln Gordon, McGeorge Bundy, Lucian Pye, and others—argued that the best policy for the United States was to encourage "economic development" in these countries, to offer them a non-communist path to wealth and power.[71] Such a program meant substantial economic aid to build up the infrastructure of these countries—roads, education, water projects, etc.—and heavy military aid to protect regimes favorable to the United States. Their program also implied covert operations that would insure "stability." In short, they asked for substantial

U.S. involvement in "development," coupled with heavy military aid to pro-U.S. governments designed to insure the "climate of stability" needed for development.

Selling the Threat to the Third World

It is of great importance that the American people, now well aware of the technical and scientific challenge posed by the Communist world, understand and rise to meet the equally great, and perhaps more subtly dangerous offensive which the Sino-Soviet bloc has vigorously launched in the less developed areas. This offensive represents an attempt by the Sino-Soviet bloc to employ its growing economic and industrial capacities as a means of bringing the newly developing free nations within the Communist orbit.

—C. Douglas Dillon, Deputy Undersecretary of State for Economic Affairs, speaking in 1958. Dillon, who would become Kennedy's Treasury Secretary, would seem to be exaggerating, since the "Sino-Soviet bloc" was actually, at the time he spoke, falling apart.

There were numerous problems with the developmental approach, the most important being that the very trade and currency policies being followed by the U.S. were reinforcing "underdevelopment."[72] From a political standpoint another problem was even more severe. There was no domestic political coalition within the United States that was favorable to a massive program of foreign aid. Indeed, latent American isolationism, very strong in Congress, had insured the failure of any attempts by the Eisenhower Administration to provide aid in a consistent form. Unable to sell their program on its own merits, (who could make a convincing case for Congress that foreign aid was not a massive "give-away"?) Kennedy's advisors discovered that their program was politically feasible only under one condition. If they could prove to Congress (and to the American people) that these countries were imperiled by Soviet "aggression," then the required political support for a program of foreign aid might be forthcoming. Without foreign aid, the Kennedy Administration claimed, the Cuban model would become more and more attractive to the Third World.

Kennedy's approach was, by and large, successful. Foreign aid was significantly expanded, new programs like the Alliance for Progress were established, and American foreign policy became more and more intertwined with Third World concerns. Indeed, by the end of the Kennedy-Johnson Administrations, U.S. policy was so focused on Southeast Asia that a number of eminent Europhiles, the most typical being George Ball, had come out against Vietnam policy because it was distracting the U.S. from its primary commitment: Western Europe. But Ball's was a voice in the wilderness; more typical of the Kennedy-Johnson Administrations were men like Walt Rostow. Rostow, who had taken the lead among intellectuals in arguing that the U.S.S.R. was the main threat to the Third World, failed to see that the Russians were just as concerned with stability as with revolution. True, Moscow provided arms and support for its allies in the Third World, contesting American influence wherever possible, but the Russians were also a conservative power, fearful that Third World nationalism would be difficult for them to contain. In the end, Rostow and his compatriots were projecting East-West perceptions into North-South struggles.

The second peak of anti-Soviet hostility, like the first, had a foreign policy dimension, but not one directly related to U.S.-Soviet relations. Fear of the Russians was exaggerated in order to win support for foreign aid and a Third World orientation; just as, in the first phase, it was helpful in winning support for the Marshall Plan and a European orientation. The two peaks are not similar in terms of the specific forms of foreign policy, but they are quite similar in terms of the way that negative perceptions of Soviet conduct helped build domestic support for a shift in foreign policy orientation.

Recent attempts by the Reagan Administration to warn of an imminent Soviet threat to the United States are related to yet another shift in the locus of foreign policy, this one a result of the breakdown of the consensus symbolized by Vietnam, combined with a renewed desire to project American power abroad. To understand the sharp rise in anti-Soviet rhetoric that characterizes the Reagan Administration, we must go back to the early 1970s and Richard Nixon. Nixon's Administration had been a nightmare for the Europeanists. As a legislator, Nixon had been an important cog in the Asia-first machine. His roots were in California, where European inclinations had never been strong. Even though Nixon had been "seasoned" with a New York law practice, there was no guarantee that he would accept the legacy of the Marshall Plan outlook on the world.

In three significant ways, Nixon attempted to break U.S. policy away from the Eurocapitalist vision. First, he wondered aloud about the relevance of NATO. Europeanists were shocked by Henry Kissinger's "Year of Europe" speech in 1973, in which he noted that the "United States has global interests and responsibilities. Our European allies have regional interests."[74] Kissinger was calling for a relaxation of America's preoccupation with Europe in favor of an outlook that made Europe simply one area of concern among many.

Secondly, Nixon did, in fact, apply the Asia-first mentality while president, albeit with a catch. Nixon's opening with China was proof of his determination to upgrade Asia in the strategic thinking of the United States. If one simply ignores the fact that China is governed by communists, which Nixon in his new-found ideological eclecticism was willing to do, then the new China policy was nothing other than the right-wing approach of the 1940s brought to life. China had finally been called upon to play the role that the China Lobby had demanded, only it was not the China of Chiang Kai-shek.

Finally, Nixon's foreign economic policies repudiated all the crucial notions of the Europeanists. In 1971 Nixon suspended the Bretton Woods agreements that had organized the postwar world, and took the U.S. off the gold standard. Moreover, Nixon's Secretary of the Treasury, John Connally, was an unabashed economic nationalist who favored protectionist policies and a go-it-alone mentality. Neither the integrationists of the Common Market nor the free-traders in the multinational corporations were happy with Nixon's attempt to insure the self-sufficiency of the American economy at whatever the international economic costs.

As if this were not enough, American foreign policy was in even greater disarray because of the fallout from the Vietnam War. It would seem to be true, as Leslie Gelb has argued, that Vietnam followed logically from the policies of containment elaborated during the 1940s.[75] For this very reason, the U.S. failure in that country was extremely serious, for it raised the question of whether or not containment itself was flawed. Did the U.S. "need" to commit so much to Vietnam? If one accepted the idea that the Russians were behind every Third World revolution, and that this "aggression" constituted a threat to U.S. security, then Vietnam was logical and necessary. Many experts, such as Walt Rostow, still feel that it was the right war at the right time. But if one rejects the vital interest of Vietnam to American security—as men like Clark Clifford and Paul Warnke implicitly did—then one also rejects some of the crucial components of the entire containment strategy.[76]

The American withdrawal from Vietnam stimulated a major debate in policymaking circles about the future locus of foreign policy. Some argued that only "core" areas of direct vital concern to the U.S.—especially Europe and the Middle East—required military intervention, while other areas like Africa were not worth the cost. Others argued that Vietnam was a failure of nerve on the part of the U.S., demanding an even greater commitment to the principle of cold war liberalism. The debate became extremely heated, and it burst into the public arena when the Carter Administration took office in 1977. Carter initially seemed to side with the position that emphasized a primary commitment to the core areas, and this aroused the ire of all those who believed that the problem in Vietnam was a failure of American will.

The Carter Administration came into power with two apparent objectives: restoring Europe to its central place after the shift adopted by Nixon, and developing a new U.S. stance vis-a-vis the Third World. The former task was urged most prominently by the Trilateral Commission, the ultimate voice in articulating European sympathies and closely linked to the Carter Administration in outlook and personnel. The program of the Trilateralists represented a return to the free trade principles of the late 1940s; a solidification of the NATO alliance; the creation of a new system of trade and currency to replace Bretton Woods and to supplement international trade negotiations; support for European integration; and a search for areas in which North America, Europe, and Japan could overcome petty national disputes in favor of international cooperation. It seemed like Europe versus Asia once again—only this time Japan was seen as part of the European alliance. But it was not a replay of the 1940s, for the domestic coalitions had shifted greatly since then, and these shifts help explain why Carter's foreign policy failed and why anti-Soviet perceptions increased.

Without an external threat, it is difficult to have a free trade program. In the short run, the only time period that counts in electoral politics, Americans who lose jobs and income overseas are not likely to support programs that continue such trends unless they are convinced that the aggression of an external enemy makes such sacrifice necessary. In the 1980s, for example, as debates over free trade versus protectionism dominate the Congress, the "Japanese threat" has been added to the Soviet threat as an external spectre. But the trilateralists were caught in a bind. They could not raise the issue of Japanese competition given their close ties to Japan, leaving them only a Soviet threat to cultivate. To a minor extent, they did; one report of the Trilateral Commission did bring back to life all the 1940s nightmares about Soviet expansion. But, by and large, the Carter Administration was unwilling to adopt without reservation the most extreme anti-Soviet perceptions. The reason had a good deal to do with the other foreign policy item on Carter's agenda: developing a post-Vietnam global strategy.

The Return of the Europeanists

...the United States government has preferred in the last few years to deal bilaterally with individual European governments and Japan, and to centralize relations on itself, as in the past, believing that this maximized its power and prolonged its leadership...

But the drawbacks of bilateralism are great. It is not surprising that the Japanese and Europeans, though of great potential importance to each other, both in themselves and in the effect they have on America, have very little sense of each other or their potential role together in the international system. The necessary development of a Europe able to speak with a single voice is made more difficult. And the United States is encouraged to underrate its partners' adaptations to a changing context. It sees itself all too easily as the only power with an adequate world view, an attitude which buttresses its unilateralism and desire to maintain the privileges of leadership, even when it is less and less able to exercise leadership responsibilities by itself...

It is in this spirit that the Trilateral Commission, with participants from North America, Japan and the European Community, has been set up to propose jointly considered contributions by their nations to the major international issues that confront mankind.

Trilateral Commission, *The Crisis of International Cooperation* (1973).

The pro-Europeanists around Carter—such as Cyrus Vance—were convinced that the U.S. overextended itself in Vietnam. They were strong believers in the notion that the U.S. should concern itself most explicitly with core areas like Europe and the Middle

East, relying on non-interventionary solutions in other parts of the world, especially Africa. Their problem, therefore, was as follows. If they aroused the spectre of the Soviet threat, they put themselves in the position of alienating their foreign policy toward the Third World as well as risking the antagonism of Europe, since the Europeans had come to depend on the Soviet Union for trade. Make the Cold War rhetoric too strong, Carter discovered, and trilateralism went by the board. But make trilateralism too dominant, he also found, and without the Soviet threat his administration would increasingly lose political popularity. This dilemma was one that Carter could never overcome. He pursued both policies at once, an economically oriented trilateralism and, toward the end of his term, a militarily oriented Cold War, but he was unable to obtain either. The third peak of the Soviet threat began under Carter, but did not reach its full height until a new administration came to power.

Carter's problem, in a word, was that conditions had changed drastically since the Marshall Plan. In the late 1940s, a pro-European free trade policy literally demanded the cultivation of the Soviet threat. But in the late 1970s, the exact opposite was taking place. Now, given the increasing political and economic power of Europe, plus changes in the world's balance of power, to be pro-Europe was to question the most extreme anti-Soviet statements. Similarly, a generation ago the right-wing of the Republican Party, Asia-oriented and isolationist in inclination, opposed the installation of the Cold War, but by 1980, if the Reagan Administration is typical, West Coast conservative Republicanism, still suspicious of Europe and pro-Asia, had come to believe in the Soviet threat to an even greater degree than its traditional domestic antagonist.

The foreign policy coalition that has come together around Ronald Reagan is not totally anti-European. There are still confirmed cold warriors like Paul Nitze with roots in the anti-communist consensus of the late 1940s, and some of the support for Reagan's hard line against the Russians comes from pro-Israel politicians with links to Europe. Given the economic importance of Europe, no administration can afford to ignore the area. Nonetheless, Reagan's foreign policy coalition can be seen as the delayed triumph of an Asia-first mentality, but under conditions that forced it to adopt extremely negative perceptions of Soviet conduct.

From the perspective of the Reagan Administration, the U.S. defeat in Vietnam, combined with the damage to the economy suffered by the oil shocks of the 1970s, demands a full military build-up of American forces. This build-up, the Administration claims, is due to the fact that the Soviets modernized all their forces while the U.S. stood still. But if that allegation is not true, and there is no evidence that America stood by for a decade and let the Soviets gain strategic superiority, then the Cold War militarism of the Reagan Administration must have another rationale. That rationale, in my view, can be found in the attempt of the Reagan Administration to dominate Europe economically while increasing the ability of U.S. corporations to extend their power around the globe.

The Cold War Returns

Our interests are global and they conflict with those of the Soviet Union, a state which pursues world policies most unfriendly to our own. The Soviet Union maintains the most heavily armed military establishment in history and possesses the capability to project its military forces far beyond its own borders. It's a given that, of course, we have vital interests around the world, including maritime sea lanes of communication. The hard fact is that the military power of the Soviet Union is now able to threaten these vital interests as never before. The Soviet Union also complements its direct military capabilities with proxy forces and surrogates with extensive arms sales and grants by manipulation of terrorist and subversive organizations, and through support to a number of insurgencies and separatist movements—providing arms, advice, military training, political backing.

Our military forces and those of our allies must protect our common interests in our increasingly turbulent environment. We must be prepared to deter attack and to defeat such attack when deterrence fails.

In this respect, the modernization of our strategic nuclear forces will receive first priority in our efforts to rebuild the military capabilities of the United States.

—Remarks of Judge William Clark, National Security Advisor to the President. Center for Strategic and International Studies, Georgetown University, May 21, 1982.

There are two aspects to the Reagan Administration's approach to East-West affairs, and they contradict each other. On the one hand, the U.S. is waging a geo-strategic war against the Soviet Union which requires European cooperation. On the other, the U.S. is waging an economic war against Europe that, ironically, demands a form of Soviet compliance. For the Europeans to agree to Washington's demands to increase military spending and to stop trading with the Russians would involve the loss of jobs and slowing of economic growth in Western Europe, which no incumbent government, conservative or socialist, can accept. The only way this strategy can be successful is if the Russians cooperate by being aggressive and threatening. The lack of Soviet cooperation makes it difficult for the Administration to impose its will on Western Europe, leading to a major conundrum: to the degree that Reagan intensifies the Cold War, he risks alienating Western Europe; to the degree that he seeks European cooperation against the Soviets, he undermines America's economic domination of the continent. Like the Carter Administration, Reagan faces problems whichever way he turns; unlike Carter, he has in general decided to resolve these dilemmas by explicitly moving toward a Cold War posture, although occasional concessions to Western Europe such as revoking sanctions against firms supplying the Siberian pipeline are sometimes thrown in.

"Frankly, Europe does not matter that much to us economically. It's the Eastern of "Pacific Rim" countries that will be increasingly important to us technologically and economically. China, with a billion people, is much more important than Europe. The case isn't compelling that we have to defend Europe at the risk of our own population."

Henry R. Breck, chairman and chief executive officer of Lehman Management Company and former CIA officer, speaking at the Lehrman Institute, 1983.

A major reason why the Reagan Administration has been willing to risk confrontation with European leaders is the feeling on the part of these men that Europe may not be as crucial to the future health of American corporations as Asia and other parts of the non-European world. As corporations become multinational, as the division of labor becomes global, and as scarce resources located in every continent become essential for continued production, the key to American strength, or at least to the strength of American firms, lies in their ability to operate on a global scale, shifting jobs from one place to another, obtaining what they need at the best possible price. In an unstable world, the Reagan Administration seems to believe the best guarantee of one's ability to maneuver is the possession of military force sufficient to protect one's global interests. A military build-up, while it may undermine the domestic economic strength of the U.S., also strengthens the hand of U.S. corporations in what is increasingly becoming a strife-torn world.

But military power is useless unless others accept it as unquestioned. From the Reagan Administration's perspective, U.S. power in the world has declined since the days when America could threaten, without challenge from the Soviet Union, governments around the world that pursued independent policies. Longing for the days when parity was a term that applied only to the farm belt, not to East-West military balance, the Reagan Administration seems determined, not to match the Soviets, but to surpass them. Members of the Administration are convinced of the following propositions: (1) there *is* such a thing as strategic superiority; (2) the U.S. can obtain it; and (3) once obtained, it will enable America to pursue its own self-interest multilaterally without needing the support of squeamish allies without having to kow tow to other superpowers. The program is ambitious, but its direction is clear. For the Reagan Administration to have any success in moving away from trilateralism to unilateralism, in short, the articulation of a Soviet menace is absolutely essential.

Ronald Reagan's foreign policy confirms the argument of this chapter, that external events are crucial to perceptions of the Soviet threat, but that those events do not necessarily involve the Soviet Union directly. I have suggested here that since 1945, factions within foreign policy coalitions have used the Soviet threat to shift American foreign policy from one direction to another. In the first Cold War, the Asia-firsters were vanquished and a pro-European policy was organized around the Soviet threat. The second peak of anti-Soviet hostility occurred at a time when the U.S. sought the capacity to intervene in revolutionary struggles taking place in the Third World. Now, after a decade of indecision, global turmoil, and power-sharing, the Reagan Administration seems set on undermining trilateralism and pursuing a foreign policy rooted in nationalistic and unilateral sympathies. The cycle has been completed. Thirty years ago a cultivation of the Soviet threat was a key element in moving the U.S. from unilateral isolationism to pan-

European cooperation. In the present context, the same Soviet threat becomes the linch-pin of a strategy to take the U.S. away from multilateral cooperation in favor of go-it-alone nationalism. The world in thirty years changed drastically; the role played by the Soviet threat in shifting the perspective of American foreign policy changed hardly at all.

These reflections suggest that while foreign policy issues are important to understanding the rise and fall of negative perceptions of Soviet conduct, they are not always issues that directly concern the Soviet Union. Distilling the debates over the orientation of U.S. foreign policy produces the following conclusions:

1. Negative perceptions of Soviet intentions increase when existing foreign policy coalitions are in disarray and when new coalitions seek to push foreign policy in a new direction.

2. The first peak of anti-Soviet sentiment was related to attempts to give American foreign policy a European orientation; the second peak was part of a campaign to enhance the importance of the Third World; and the last is a product of the collapse of the Cold War liberal consensus after Vietnam and Nixon. But in all these cases it was the domestic side of the foreign policy coalition that was responsible for the increase in the perception of the Soviet threat, not specific aspects of U.S.-Soviet relations.

3. In general, the Soviet threat is used by an incumbent administration because its real objectives are not especially popular. Americans were not inclined to accept the free trade notions of elite bankers in the late 1940s unless the reconstruction of a European-oriented economy were rationalized under a threat from the Russians. Kennedy's plans for a global intervention capacity ran counter to historic American isolationism, necessitating that they be recast to meet an alleged Soviet threat in the Third World. Reagan's military adventurism and nationalism strike a popular chord but have also met residual distrust when put into practice; claims that the Soviets have radically outspent the U.S. on military hardware are essential if Reagan's other objectives are to be met.

4. It follows that an administration honest about its intentions would not need to exaggerate the Soviet threat. That state of affairs will only come about when the American people pay more attention to the world, demanding from their politicians that they be held accountable for their acts. In this sense, a contributing cause of the persistence of the Soviet threat in the U.S. is the low level of awareness and parochialism of public discussion of foreign policy so characteristic of American domestic politics.

CHAPTER VII

ECONOMIC TRANSFORMATIONS AND ANTI-SOVIET HOSTILITY

Numerous theories have been proposed about the relationship between the defense budget and the economy. Paul Baran and Paul Sweezy, for example, argue that huge defense expenditures are necessary to absorb the "surplus" generated by capitalism, which produces much more than it can consume and therefore requires tremendous waste.[77] Seymour Melman, on the other hand, maintains that defense spending is a drain on economic growth, that far from being necessary (as Baran and Sweezy imply), it is not in the best interests of American capitalism.[78] Other writers argue that imperialism is essential to the performance of the American economy, and that the maintenance of an imperial system requires large-scale defense expenditures whatever the state of the domestic economy.[79]

There are elements of truth to all these theories, but all of them are also static; they assume little variation in the pattern of defense spending. Yet, as I argued in Chapter II, negative perceptions of an external enemy rise and fall, and as they do, the size of the defense budget goes up and down. Therefore it is essential to determine whether there are similar economic transformations taking place during each of the three peaks of anti-Soviet perceptions, and whether these periods are different from the two valleys. In this chapter, I will argue that the peak periods were times in which political coalitions were arguing for a strategy of macroeconomic growth and found the use of the defense budget the most politically acceptable way of trying to effectuate that result.

First it is worth noting that there is a relationship between overall economic conditions and the rise of the Soviet threat, but it is not the relationship that one might immediately expect. Negative perceptions of Soviet intentions generally peak after periods of recession, not during them. This is because increased military spending is as much *political* as economic, designed to solidify growth coalitions oriented to domestic and international expansion.

In 1946, economists of every conceivable political stripe expected a letdown after the tremendous productive outpouring of World War II. Truman's economic advisors, especially activists like Leon Keyserling of the Council of Economic Advisors, saw defense spending as a good way to avoid the expected recession. Indeed, NSC-68, in which Keyserling and his aides participated, recommended defense spending as a way of enhancing the economic growth of the United States. The only problem was that by the time NSC-68 was written, 1950, the postwar recessionary expectations had already passed. With the economy beginning its long postwar boom, the rise in defense spending that took place in the early 1950s was no longer "needed" to bring the country out of a trough.

Similarly, the books by Maxwell Taylor and Henry Kissinger that began the full-scale assault on Eisenhower's foreign policy and produced the second wave of anti-Soviet perceptions were published at a time when the economy had entered its biggest slowdown since the Depression. Reluctant to follow an activist macroeconomic course, Eisenhower's domestic policymakers were most worried about inflation and attempted to cool down the economy when they concluded that economic growth was getting out of hand. By 1957, when the Taylor and Kissinger books were being written, the Eisenhower Administration had produced a situation in which both inflation and unemployment were high. The foreign policy activists who were so critical of Eisenhower's "New Look" pointed out that the economy would benefit from increased defense spending. Yet by the time they had an impact, in the first two years of the Kennedy Administration, the economy had recovered and was in the process of racking up its best growth record in the postwar period. Once again, increased expenditures for defense took place after the recession, not during it.

Recent experience also conforms to this pattern. Since 1968 there has been a substantial downturn in the American economy. For most of this time, while Republicans were president, slowed economic growth was not necessarily seen as a bad thing. There were some economists, however, who felt that the fall-off in defense spending under Nixon and Ford could not be allowed to continue. But even as the Carter Administration came into office and began to increase defense spending, the worst aspects of the recession had passed. Another one would arrive in 1981-82, this time coinciding with the Reagan Administration's plans to throw money at the military, something Reagan would have done in any case, recession or not.

Because increases in defense spending come after recessions, one cannot make a simple correlation between overall levels of economic performance and the rise and fall of anti-Soviet percep-tions. It is true that the first tremors of a new build-up of hard-line views toward the Soviet Union occur during times of economic difficulty. But by the time these sentiments are converted into higher defense expenditures, the "need" for the economic stimu-lant has passed. This suggests that one must enrich an economic understanding of the problem with a political analysis, that politi-cal economy, and not economics *per se*, helps explain the rise and fall of negative perceptions of the Soviet Union.

Support for the Cold War on the part of major manufacturers and large-scale labor unions has been close to axiomatic in the postwar period. A very strong political coalition that lobbies in favor of increased defense spending has come into existence, and, in order to make the case for a higher military budget, it relies on the cultivation of an external threat. Indeed, sometimes the percep-tions of a hostile enemy and the profits that accrue from the defense budget are so blatant as to be embarrassing. When both corporations and unions have a direct stake in the military budget, they cannot but make the claim that America needs a greater defense effort; it is economic suicide not to.

The fact that the military budget is an indirect means of sustaining profits and jobs is important to note, for it helps explain the persistence of anti-Soviet sentiments. But it does not explain why those sentiments rise and fall. The answer to that question lies in the nature of political coalitions that organize to promote eco-nomic growth.

One pattern that emerges in each peak period of anti-Soviet hostility is that a governing coalition comes into power based upon promises to the working class, minorities, and other disadvantaged groups. Many politicians, especially Democrats, find that they must make such promises in order to be elected. Once in power, when faced with the choice of taking from the rich or trying to expand the whole pie, they invariably choose the latter, since it is politically more acceptable. And when they try to expand the size of the economy, they discover that the public budget is an important source of economic growth. Committing themselves to an expansion of the budget, they further discover that among the many ways to spend the public's money, defense spending is the least controversial. Unlike public housing or medical care, which arouse the ire of private companies that provide those services for profit, defense spending has no direct opposition in the private sector. Indeed the opposite is true, for defense spending has created a sector all its own which needs increased spending. Consequently, there is enormous pressure on politicians to stimulate macroeconmoic growth by using the defense budget. The purpose is not the short term goal of taking the economy out of recession, but a future-oriented goal of sustaining a growth coalition organized around spending in order to expand the economy so that those at the bottom will be able to obtain more without detracting from the privileges of those at the top.

Alternatively, it is also clear that the valleys in hostility toward external enemies come when growth coalitions are not in power. Republican presidents generally do not made extensive promises to working class people and minorities about enhanced social benefits. They often try to campaign on the fear of inflation, which is of more direct concern to middle class people, or on the basis of highly symbolic, non-economic issues like crime or national prestige. Not having committed themselves to deliver on promises, the resulting coalitions need not fuel extensive economic growth. In fact, Republican coalitions often try to slow down the rate of growth in order to bring inflation under control. Thus they do not need nor want growth in the public budget, and they make an attempt to bring federal spending, including defense spending, under control. This also means lower taxes, an attractive campaign promise to the middle class. Under these conditions, negative perceptions of an external enemy decrease under political coaltions that are opposed to federally sponsored macroeconomic growth.

Both the Truman and Kennedy periods confirm the relation between macroeconomic growth coalitions and the rise of the Soviet threat. Truman, for example, while personally not convinced of the notion that federal spending was good for the expansion of the economy, brought into policymaking circles Leon Keyeserling, who believed in the idea very much. Keyserling was a domestic liberal who urged extensive governmental programs in housing and medical care. He was also a foreign policy activist who wanted to expand defense spending. (Keyserling is currently on the board of the Committee on the Present Danger.) When Truman's plans for public housing were scuttled by the real estate lobby and when his medical care plan was devastated by the American Medical Association, defense spending became the most attractive option to bring about continued economic growth. Keyserling, who was the second Chairman of the Council of Economic Advisors, wrote, along with his staff, the economic sections of NSC-68. That document noted that "The United States...is allocating only about 20 percent of its resources to defense and investment (or 22 percent including foreign assistance), and little of its investment outlays are directed to war-supporting industries. In an emergency the United States could allocate more than 50 percent of its resources to military purposes and foreign assistance, or five to six times as much as present."[80] This was a sign that increased federal spending on a vast scale was possible. Although Truman personally opposed so ambitious a program, the ground was laid for using the defense budget as a politically acceptable means of effectuating economic growth.

The situation had become clearer by the time that Kennedy took office. Kennedy's entire campaign had been oriented around a plea to move the country, which was generally interpreted as a plea for more rapid economic growth. There are two general ways to achieve such growth. One is for the government to create it by spending a great deal, sending ripples through the economy, and producing a multiplier effect that would lead to increased production. Few doubt that such a program works; the conservative argument against it is merely that the costs (inflation, inefficiency, whatever) would be greater than the benefits. Their alternative method is for the government to encourage business to invest more actively. Inducements such as tax cuts, subsidies, and favorable trade terms have generally been used toward that end.

Kennedy, as a centrist president, tried both approaches. Aware of those to his right, the president, particularly after his confrontation with the steel industry, "simply did not want another fight with business," as Arthur Schlesinger, Jr. has put it.[81] The question facing the Administration was how to achieve economic growth without antagonizing business. The president therefore chose to rely on indirect measures, such as a tax cut to stimulate consumer spending or an investment tax credit to urge business to invest.

But Kennedy could not rely on indirect measures only, for they do not have controllable impacts on overall growth levels. As a result, the new administration also paid attention to using the federal budget as an economic stimulant. This raised the opposition of business. But when big business denounces government spending, which it does reflexively, it announces opposition, not to spending *per se* (businesspeople want federal spending that sub sidizes them) but to programs that redistribute income. Defense spending, Kennedy discovered, is one of the few major spending programs that does not arouse business opposition—space exploration was another. Thus Kennedy was able to use government to stimulate economic growth without raising conservative ire.

Defense spending has a variety of economic impacts. Generally, federal spending on defense works to the benefit of the largest firms. It also forces the economy to reorganize itself along advanced technological lines, to the advantage of those (already large) companies that can afford the costs of increasingly capital-intensive machinery. In addition, the large outlays of federal monies encourage those who already have the greatest political power to try and take a larger share, thus favoring firms that have sufficient size to maintain a large Washington effort at lobbying. The impact of these centralizing tendencies is that each spurt of defense spending strengthens those non-market oriented monopolies that can mobilize themselves to push for greater share of the *next* round of defense spending. In short, when the spectre of an external threat is raised in one period as a means of increasing defense spending, it lays the foundation for raising the same spectre in the next period. Kennedy relied on defense spending to stimulate the economy because previous presidents had done so, making the defense production sector so powerful that no president can ignore it.

By the time of the third peak in anti-Soviet hostility, the relationship between growth politicians in power and a rise in foreign policy aggressiveness continued, but in a new form. No longer are the Democrats the party that calls for rapid and extensive economic growth; that rhetoric shifted to the Republican Party, and as it did, the most negative perceptions of the Soviet Union shifted along with it.

We cannot understand the most recent outbreak of Cold War sentiment in the United States—as well as the reasons why it has already begun to peak—without considering the remarkable economic plight that gripped the advanced capitalist West in the 1970s. Accustomed to economic growth as if by right, the United States was politically unprepared to enter a period of deep and persistent stagflation, in which rising prices can only be checked by slowing economic activity to a minimum. Interestingly enough, the Nixon Administration—based on a traditional Republican commitment to balanced budgets—did attempt to bring defense spending under control and also took steps in the international economy which recognized, however tentatively, that economic austerity demanded reform of traditional American practices. When the Republicans left office in 1976, the question facing their successor was whether the United States would go backwards to its growth-oriented politics of old or attempt to continue a program of lower military spending and economic restraint.

Jimmy Carter was caught smack in the middle of this dilemma. On the one hand, Carter's economic advisors, especially those associated with the Trilateral Commission, recognized that a new era had dawned. When candidate Carter called for sharp cuts in the military budget—the exact amount was disputed from the start—he was speaking the language of fiscal conservatism once associated with the Republican Party. Indeed much of the Carter Administration was quasi-Republican, including its foreign policy. Especially in the first two years of his presidency, Carter seemed to be another Eisenhower, cautious about foreign intervention, speaking of the limits of American power, and asking for more responsible, less bloated, military budgets. It was the economically correct strategy to follow. Unfortunately for Carter, it also produced disastrous political consequences.

As the elections of 1980 drew closer, a pronounced shift in the priorities of the Carter Administration could be observed. Suddenly the Administration was calling for increases in military spending and seemed anxious to demonstrate to the world, or at least to itself, that it was not afraid to use American forces somewhere around the globe. What had happened? Obviously, external events like the hostage kidnapping in Iran and the Soviet invasion of Afghanistan played a significant role in this changing consciousness. But it would be drastically incorrect to ignore the role that economic factors played in developing strategies to combat the recession of the 1970s.

In the past, the major platform of the Democratic Party had been to stimulate growth through public works and since, as I have argued in this chapter, military spending was the politically "safest" way to spend the taxpayers' money, the Democrats had become the part of the Cold War. Safely within the Democratic Party during the Carter years were such Cold War liberals as Senators Daniel Patrick Moynihan and Henry Jackson who both argued that the Democrats could still be the party of guns and butter. These men recognized what Carter only belatedly under-stood, which was that in order to obtain the votes of working class Americans, no party could stand for economic austerity. In order to secure his position within the party, Carter moved sharply into a new political position within the party, and when only significant opposition to his renomination came from Edward Kennedy, Carter was in a better position to secure his right flank. Unexpectedly, Jimmy Carter was renominated, and at least in part, his success was due to his born-again conversion to the first principles of his party: economic growth through military expenditure.

Although a return to fundamentals helped Carter win the nomination, it did not enable him to secure reelection. To under-stand why, we must confront the fact that 1980 signified a major transformation in American politics, not over the goals of the society, but over the party chosen by the voters to meet those goals.

Ronald Reagan could never become president, it seems safe to say, if he had run in 1980 on a traditional Republican platform of a balanced budget achieved through economic restraint. As Carter's Republican phase made clear, that was not the message the voters wanted to hear. Instead, Reagan, knowing full well that without working class votes his campaign was doomed, adopted the growth strategy that had worked so well in the past for the Democrats. Supply-side economics which, when the Democrats were in power, was called Keynesianism, gave the Republican candidate the chance to enter working class cities like Buffalo claiming to promise jobs. Reagan was elected in large measure because he made a credible case that his economic program would restore prosperity.

For Reagan, as for the Democrats, the problem was not to make promises but to carry them out. Reagan's economic advisors convinced him that a tax cut need not necessarily produce huge deficits, since it would unleash economic activity that would in turn increase revenues to the Federal government. Therefore, the supply-siders happily concluded, Reagan could also raise the military budget without worrying about whether the funds would be available to pay for it. It was only a matter of time before tax cuts and military spending would support each other.

This was good news for Mr. Reagan, since not only was he committed to an expansion of business influence, but he was also dead-set on furbishing America's military apparatus. In this, his economics and his foreign policy were linked as they were under John F. Kennedy. In the worldview of the Reagan Administration, tax cuts would finance growth which would finance the military, while military spending would finance growth which would permit tax cuts. In short, Reaganism saw once more the interconnection of a growth strategy and the Soviet threat, since the latter was viewed as necessary to support the former. The economic factors underlying the third peak in the Cold War were once again crucial, even if this time they coalesced under the Republicans, no longer under the Democrats.

Yet economic conditions in the United States have changed drastically since the time that tax cuts and military spending worked to benefit each other under John F. Kennedy. No sooner did Mr. Reagan obtain his program from Congress than the enormous contradictions in his perspective began to reveal themselves. Congress cut taxes, but instead of stimulating growth, the resulting deficits kept interest rates high, which slowed the economy down. Under these conditions, raising the military budget meant one of two choices, neither palatable: further cuts in domestic spending, especially in Social Security; or repudiating of tax cut in order to hold the deficits in line. The Reagan Administration, one year after the triumph of supply-side economics, was forced to repudiate supply-side economics and to seek a tax increase. And even with the increase in taxes, pressures to balance the budget were so enormous that in the summer of 1982, Congress passed its first veto of a Reagan action by passing an appropriations bill that favored cuts in military spending over continued chopping of social program. The Reagan agenda was not working, and as the economic costs of the third Cold War came home to the American people, political pressure to curtail military spending became as strong as earlier pressure to increase it. Under tight economic circumstances, a relaxation of some of the more extreme versions of the Soviet threat will inevitably occur; the U.S. economy cannot pay for what U.S. rhetoric demands. Capitalist economics, in other words, has as much to do with explaining why anti-Soviet sentiment wanes as it does with how it waxes.

Thus, the Reagan years leave an ambiguous legacy. On the one hand, the Administration has not retreated one inch in its attempt to portray the Soviet Union as the greatest evil existing on earth. In Congressional testimony and in public speeches, Reagan Administration spokespeople still use the language and imagery of groups like the Committee on the Present Danger. But like all previous Administrations, this one finds that the language used for domestic consumption cannot be used for foreign policy. As Reagan and his advisors stare at a West European revolt, deficits accumulating into the sunset, and public opinion polls, it knows that there is no alternative but to seek at least some limited bipolar negotiations with the Soviet leadership. As it entered the 1984 elections, the

Reagan Administration began to soften the rhetoric toward the Soviet Union, repudiating its own initially hostile language. There is a limit, in short, to how anti-Soviet even this administration can be, a limit that has already been reached. The third wave of anti-Soviet hysteria since World War II peaked in early 1983 and is not likely to return until the next cycle begins.

Clearly, one must consider domestic economic factors in trying to explain why hostile perceptions of the Soviet Union increase at some times more than others. Some of them can be summarized as follows:

1. Often the first stirrings of a new wave of anti-Soviet perceptions will originate in recessionary times, or times when a recession is expected. But one cannot conclude from this that there is necessarily a direct intent to use the Soviet threat to increase the defense budget, for by the time the threat translated into hard dollars, the recession has generally passed.

2. It is not the avoidance of recession but the attempt to create a macroeconomic strategy of economic growth that best explains the rise of anti-Soviet perceptions. The perceived threat from the Soviet Union increases when activist domestic coalitions come to power. These coalitions, usually organized by the Democratic Party, promise benefits to those on the lower end of the economic scale, which they hope to pay off through an overall expansion of the economy. (The alternative to expansion is taking from the higher rungs, which courts political danger.) As they search for politically safe measures of expanding the budget, such administrations inevitably discover the defense budget, for, unlike social welfare, defense spending does not redistribute income, and therefore does not arouse opposition from businesspeople and conservatives. In this sense, increases in the perception of an external enemy are associated with attempts to raise the defense budget. Although it would be hard to trace a direct causal link between growth strategies and deliberate manipulation of perceptions of Soviet intentions, there are definitely periods in which economic needs and foreign policy perceptions of Soviet intentions work to support each other.

3. Alternatively, perceptions of the Soviet threat decline when an administration is in power that is not attracted to economic growth, for it has not made any promises to the poor and the powerless that it has to pay off. Indeed, if anything, such anti-growth coalitions fear a rise in foreign policy hostility, for that might mean inflationary budgets and the necessity to raise taxes.

4. In recent years the impetus to a growth strategy has shifted from the Democrats to the Republicans, but as this shift takes place

the contradictions of growth politics change as well. In times of austerity, one cannot offer tax cuts and the Cold War as well. There is overwhelming pressure to choose one or the other. When Americans find out how much it costs to keep the Soviet threat alive, they weaken perceptibly in their commitment to military spending, and when that happens, the most negative perceptions of Soviet conduct tend to recede.

CHAPTER VIII

IN SEARCH OF AN EXPLANATION

Unlike most books on the Cold War, this one has emphasized domestic politics, not international relations, as a major source of superpower tensions. My focus has been on such political factors as the nature of electoral competition, the struggle between different branches of government, intrabureaucratic fighting, and policy disputes over economics and foreign affairs. All of these features, in one way or another, stress the political features of liberal democracy over the economic features of capitalism. Since this kind of explanation is so different from those generally advanced on the left, some elaboration may be helpful. What is it about the kind of democracy the U.S. practices—a democracy so far from perfect— that lends itself so easily to the manipulation of external threats? U.S. society is, internally, far more open and attractive than Soviet society, yet its foreign policy is so often bombastic, parochial, and destabilizing. Are democracy and militarism linked? Why is U.S. foreign policy more simplistic near election time and more responsible between elections? One cannot understand why Americans are susceptible to extreme hysteria about the Soviet threat without understanding what has gone wrong with democracy in the U.S., just as one cannot understand the substitution of patriotism for

---

* This chapter is a revised and edited version of the author's "Perverse Politics and the Cold War," in *New Left Review*, "Exterminism and Cold War" (London: Verso, 1982), 227-260.

internationalism in the Soviet Union without discussing the per-version of already existing socialism. The Cold War is, in short, an affair of states, and to understand it, one must begin with an analysis of the modern state.

States gather power in order to carry out, within a spatially or otherwise delimited arena, tasks that the individuals composing that arena cannot carry out themselves. Individuals can do many things that states have difficulty accomplishing, like producing art or innovating—hence, in the West, the praise of individualism and the distrust of government. Yet, bourgeois ideology to the contrary, there are also tasks which states carry out that individuals would only botch—hence, in the East, the reification of the state and the denigration of the person. Marxism and liberalism, each in its own way, have focused on the accumulation of capital, by and large an affair of private persons or groups. Such understanding must be complemented with a focus on the accumulation of power, by and large an affair of public agencies.

Of all the forms of collective action, two have characterized the modern world and have formed the character of the modern state. One is economic growth, the other is preparation for war. Neither can be accomplished by individual effort alone, though both require individual acts. To sponsor growth and protect national security, states have developed extraordinary powers to steer or direct collective action toward the accomplishment of collectively defined ends.

Growth is a phenomenon so ubiquitous that, once introduced into economic life, there seems to be no stopping its force. In the name of growth, capitalism was given a free hand, socialism consolidated its power, and development became the highest priority of the underdeveloped. There is no society where the allure of growth has been contained, none, at least in the modern world, where greater material prosperity has been deliberately and consciously rejected as costing more than it is worth. States differ, sometimes violently, over how to achieve growth; they vary not at all over whether to achieve it. To be modern is to want more.

While capital accumulation requires individual effort, growth, understood as an overall process, demands collective planning. Socialist bloc countries and Third World economies, short of time, understand this implicitly and proceed toward the objective of growth with blunt instruments, including terror and forced collectivization. Yet even the capitalist road, while praising the individual, requires planning to achieve the objective of growth. In some cases this planning is undertaken by "private" corporations so large, integrated, and authoritative that they assume the character of states. In other cases the way is paved by indicative planning and efforts to convince individual actors to mesh their objectives into common ends. In no case is the pursuit of growth left to unplanned acts fashioned by an impersonal process called the market. A growing society, whatever it calls itself, will be one that consolidates unprecedented political power for the sake of encouraging that growth.

When they are not sponsoring expansion, modern states spend the bulk of their remaining time (and budget) preparing for war. No state in the modern world avoids planning for war. Militarism has been transformed from a somewhat sporadic affair of the aristocracy into an integral feature of political life affecting all. Tolstoy's ability to separate completely the action in the field from the conversation in the parlors is as irrelevant to the way the Soviet Union plans for war as James Fenimore Cooper's isolation of military virtues to the wilderness is to the United States. A modern state always contemplates violence, all the time. Some states have been able to contain the military and to limit its influence within specific sectors of society. Others have become what Harold D. Lasswell prophetically called "garrison states," bending all other social objectives to accord with militarist considerations.[82] It matters greatly whether society controls or is controlled by its military component, but it is a measure of how much the modern state plans for war that no society can escape the problem. In a century of total war, total planning for war becomes a bureaucratic routine.

More than growth, war has become, as Randolph Bourne understood, the health of the state.[83] World War I, the focus of Bourne's attention, had more to do with the building of the modern state than any other event. "Neither race had won, nor could win, the War," the British poet Edmund Blunden wrote. "The War had won, and would go on winning."[84] In the West, the war won by transforming the political economy of production. Corporate liberalism, centralized finance, the recognition of working class demands, the welfare state, economic concentration—advanced capitalism, in a word—were the product, not only of class struggle, but also of war.[85] At the same time, the war simultaneously weakened international socialism and substituted socialism in one country; advanced socialism was as much a product of the war as advanced capitalism. After this war, and to the present day, neither democracy nor socialism would ever be the same. Lincoln Steffens thought he saw in the Russian Revolution our fate. One war later, General Cummings, in Norman Mailer's *The Naked and the Dead,* saw it more clearly. "You can consider the Army, Robert," he told Lt. Hearn, "as a preview of the future."[86]

Sponsoring growth and planning for war intersect with each other at all points. A growing society is one that has more resources to be turned into war preparation, while a militarized society is one that, at some level, seeks to channel its garrison industries into growth. Those states which can accumulate the greatest amount of power are those that can expand their economies and increase their armaments. The U.S. and Russia have accumulated super power, in part, because both have married the intangible factor of ideology to the tangible reality of state machinery. The United States, the most "democratic" of the societies of the West, harnessed fantastic mass energy for assembling power to accomplish its objectives. The Soviet Union, the most "socialist" of the societies of the East, possessed the personnel and bureaucracy for assembling state power to achieve its objectives. The Cold War exists between two mobilized peoples, one mobilized behind the most progressive ideology of the nineteenth century, the other behind the most advanced ideology of the twentieth.

Democracy and socialism were instrumental in helping the United States and the Soviet Union grow and prepare for war. Yet in the process of building state power, both democracy and socialism would be transformed into something entirely new. In the United States, the dictates of growth and war mutilated democracy into something that Thomas Jefferson would never recognize, though Alexander Hamilton would. In the Soviet Union, socialism as an instrument of war and growth created a form of state power not only unrecognizable in Marx, but in fundamental ways counter to him. Democracy, at least that variety now practiced in the United States, has become a major cause for the perpetuation of the Cold War; any elite fraction wishing to pursue a policy of militarization finds it relatively easy to fan the flames of popular discontent behind an arms build-up. Socialism, at least that variety now practiced in the Soviet Union, is also responsible for the permanence of the Cold War; socialism is both the official ideology of the Russian empire and the organizing logic of its mode of war production. To discover how and why the two most liberating doctrines of the modern world were turned into support for Cold War proclivities is the purpose of the remainder of this chapter.

Democracy is a process, a noun that needs an adjective to complete the thought. In the United States, two conceptions of democracy have competed with each other since the Articles of Confederation, one based upon the notion of a republic, the other seeking to harness democratic energies for modernist expansion.

A republican form of government, as envisioned by its eighteenth century advocates, would be small-scale, localist (even agrarian), pacifistic, virtuous, and elitist. Rooted in antiquity, republicans sought in democracy a model by which proper middle-class citizens would decide, hopefully through face to face contract, their common fate. A democratic republic, in short, would be thoughtful, deliberate, and stable, incompatible either with rapid industrialization or with preparations for war. Modernizing elites, at least since Hamilton, sought, on the contrary, a nationalistic, bellicose, growing dynamic polity, one that would use the state for the purpose of industrial and military expansion. Continuously blocked at the local level, and in the halls of legislative institutions that gave disproportionate power to regional interests, nationalists needed a device to overcome republican resistance to their dreams of modernization. As I argue elsewhere, a mass mobilizing conception of democracy enabled modernizing elites to fashion an alliance with a plebiscitary mass, squeezing out the localists in the middle.[87] When democratic energies were linked to modernizing tendencies, a new form of democracy was created: popular, short-tempered, easily manipulable, demagogic. Perverse democracy was a product of the need for modernizing elites to sponsor war and growth in the face of local resistance.

As Walter Karp has argued, the key turning point in the defeat of the republican alternative was the period between the Spanish American War and the outbreak of World War I.[88] During those years, modernizing leaders like Theodore Roosevelt and Woodrow Wilson learned the art of mobilizing popular passion in order to achieve concrete politico-economic changes in the American state. War, in short, has been an essential ingredient in transforming democratic republicanism into perverse democracy.

The spread of war and the growth of perverse democracy have proceeded in tandem. Each step in the advancement of suffrage, and each expansion of the scope of state activity, has been paved by a war about to be fought or rewarded for a war just concluded. No other single factor in this century has contributed as much to the expansion of political participation as the need to assemble vast numbers of working class and farm youth, from every corner of the society, for the purpose of sacrificing their lives in combat. War and perverse democracy reinforce each other. "The organization of enthusiasm,"[89] Elie Halevy's term for the manipulation unleashed by war, has become a model of public opinion dynamics in modern democracy. At the same time, war itself has spread the equalizing, uniformity-inducing features that constitute the criteria of citizenship in perverse democracy. "The military tent where they all sleep side by side," noted Theodore Roosevelt, "will rank next to the public school among the great agents of democratization."[90]

Democracy promised to the dispossessed a utopia in which the oppression of daily life would yield to the comradeship, dignity, honor, and equality of all people. To a much greater degree than is generally realized, war has come closer, if in a distorted way, to the realization of that ideal than anything experienced in peacetime. (The sense of fraternity, as its name implies, was, of course, exclusively male). War is the *civitas* of modernity, the classical ideal of a polity in which men put aside their private interests for the sake of a common good. As Marc Ferro has written about the Great War, "Far from being an ordeal, the war liberated men's energies. It was enthusiastically received by most men of military age."[91] World War I was the culmination of the nineteenth-century impulse toward equality, bent out of shape to be certain, but there for all to see. Compared to the modern corporation, also a product of this period, war offered greater democratic gratification.

When working class demands for access to political power confronted business and governmental elites after World War I, they could no longer be ignored. After a relatively brief Republican interregnum in the United States, the force of reform became a tidal wave that threatened to make extinct Republican complacency. Searching for a metaphor to make palatable the reforms of the New Deal, Franklin D. Roosevelt employed the power of wartime imagery. As the new president said in his inaugural address of March 4, 1933, "I shall ask the Congress for the one remaining instrument to meet the crisis—broad executive power to wage a war against the emergency, as great as the power that would be given to me if we were invaded by a foreign foe." As William E. Leuchtenberg noted, "The war provided a precedent for the concentration of executive authority, for the responsibility of government, for the state of the economy, and for the role of Washington as the arbiter among social groups."[92] War, which had both accepted and perverted democratic demands, would also provide the model to incorporate those demands administratively into the modern state.

When the demands of growth were added to the requirements of war, perverse democracy was advanced even further. Economic growth has not only been compatible with democracy as understood in the United States; to a significant degree, economic growth *is* democracy. For most people most of the time, democracy came to mean, not the practice of freedoms they barely understood, nor the right to vote increasingly unexercised, but the notion that material prosperity would continue to exist. The modern crisis of democracy is really a crisis of growth; in the U.S., the extension of political rights and the provision of social entitlements had become so closely tied to growth that when the latter no longer existed, no one knew how to preserve the former. An expanding economy has meant far more to the realization of democratic desires than the Bill of Rights.

The democratic state that emerged out of a half-century of unprecedented war and fabulous economic expansion bore little resemblance to the one that entered it. Considered in a plebiscitary sense, war and growth broadened democracy enormously. More people were protected against the market than ever before. The state provided benefits unheard of fifty years earlier. Women, followed by other disenfranchised groups, were given the right to vote. A sense of belonging to a national society, of participating in an integrated realm, replaced a tradition of *ad hoc* regionalism and class divisions. The quantitative scope of democracy, symbolized by rising GNP and increasing expenditures on security, was unquestionably enhanced.

Quantity, as it so often does, came at the expense of quality. Democracy, understood in the republican sense of a healthy and vibrant public life that matures and enlightens the private self, rapidly deteriorated under the imperatives of growth and war. Controversy, education, information, participation, dissent, truth— none of the subtleties of enlightened political thought could survive the crass materialism of economic expansion and the crass conformity of militarization. The modern democratic state was as broad in base as it was narrow in purpose. Rather than democratic demands fashioning the character of the state, the tasks of the state determined the permissibility of democratic demands. Public life was to be about war and growth and democracy would have to fashion itself around that. Democracy did. Indeed, a mass society composed of generally unthinking, often ignorant, complacently privatized individuals expressing their will upon decontextualized, fragmented, and impotent public agencies in an ahistorical and often contradictory manner was hardly an obstacle to the realization of growth and war, but even seemed to many the most perfect imaginable system of realizing those ends.

By the time the Cold War arrived, in other words, democracy had been completely transformed from a republican vision into a modernized revision, one perfectly adjusted to the state's war fighting and expanding tasks. Republicans had claimed that an enlightened public realm would prevent irresponsible acts. No longer. The Cold War solidified Hamilton's victory over Jefferson, as America's major contemporary neo-Hamiltonian has argued.[93] Instead of checking war and aggrandizement, democracy, in its new form, would contribute to it. The marriage between war and perverse democracy was solidified by the promise of a permanent state of international tension which would, to the delight of perverse democrats, make permanent those plebiscitary features of perverse democracy which had heretofore been temporary.

Some sense of the impact that the Cold War had on perverse democracy can be gleaned by looking at the special cabinet meeting called by Harry Truman on September 21, 1945 to discuss whether to share atomic technology with the Soviets. No other decision, one can say in retrospect, would be more important to future generations. (This writer was three years old at the time). Had the U.S. been realistic and recognized that there would be no national barriers to science, the entire Cold War might have been avoided and the nuclear arms race brought under control before it began. How did this most "democratic" of societies proceed with this most momentous of decisions? One member of the cabinet, Henry Wallace, rambled on about Mongolian animal diseases. Two others, Fred Vinson and James Forrestal, said that the Russians could not be trusted because they had an Oriental mentality. Apparently the meeting was unable to focus. "This discussion was unworthy of the subject," Dean Acheson wrote. "No one had a chance to prepare for its complexities." If the elite was confused, the general public was schizoid. Over 80 percent of the population, in a poll taken at the same time as the cabinet meeting, recognized that the U.S. monopoly on atomic secrets was about to end, most of them concluding that the Russians would soon have the bomb. Nonetheless, 70 percent of the population (and 90 percent of the Congresspeople) were opposed to cooperation with the Soviet Union.[94]

The discovery of nuclear technology revealed a tremendous gap between the technical and scientific maturity of the United States and the staggering immaturity of its political system. Such combined and uneven development has continued to make the United States one of the main perpetrators of the nuclear terror that frightens the world. If the technology were a bit less perfect, or the political system a bit more sophisticated, matters would not be as scary as they are. But when unprecedented technological brilliance is so closely married to unprecedented political ignorance, only trouble can result.

In three specific ways does the deformity of democracy as practiced in the United States contribute to the global impasse that is the Cold War. One is the trick that nuclear technology has played on democracy, a second concerns the monopoly of security possessed by the state, and the third involves the resulting lowest common denominator problem when foreign policy conflicts with public opinion.

Nuclear weapons have played a tremendous, and not especially funny, joke on democratic expectations. War and perverse democracy in the twentieth century have been intimately linked, each pursuing the other beyond its limits. Democratic demands, unrealized within the confines of class society, have, in the past, achieved a modest, if distorted, fulfillment in the excitement of battle. Yet with the discovery of nuclear weapons, democratic wars of any sort can no longer happen. Observers like Raymond Williams are correct to point out that nuclear weapons do act as a deterrent.[95] There has not been, and there cannot be a repeat of the World War II experience.[96] Nuclear weapons have made long-enduring, labor-intensive, mass-mobilizing wars obsolete. From this point forward, only two kinds of wars are possible. One is the sort of limited (though incredibly destructive) engagement symbolized by Vietnam, an elite war with little of the enthusiasm and tension-relieving sublimation of earlier efforts. The other is a nuclear engagement, guaranteeing a certain equality of death, but in no other way satisfying democratic desires.

The U.S., in other words, is in a position where war is still capable of generating a nostalgic enthusiasm for a world that has been lost, yet actual war can never satisfy the nostalgia. Sandwiched between democratic memories and high tech realities, Americans are given to the fetish of what can be called abstract belligerence—bloodthirsty in general, almost pacifistic in the particular. All polls show the same configuration; huge rhetorical support for more weapons; confrontation politics; anti-Soviet hyperbole; very little, if any, support for specific interventions, loss of life, blood sacrifice. The result is an inevitable frustration, encouraging a rampant desire for a kind of security that can never again be achieved. American democracy has not caught up with what American technology has produced. In the popular mind, war still has something to do with honor and dignity; in the technological nightmare, war is the end of everything.

Although war may be a democratic memory, the technology of nuclear war demands a secrecy and elitism totally at odds even with perverse democratic dreams. Called on to participate, but at the same time prevented from engaging in public action, the American people become spectators to the activities of their own government, bearing the same active/passive relationship to the Cold War as they do to a football game. (Indeed, the arms race is pictured in the U.S. press as a kind of sport, one side ahead in offense, the other concentrating on defense.) Unable to achieve the democratic satisfaction that war promises due to the inhibitions of nuclear weapons, Americans are ripe for the kind of routinized demagogy that passes for campaign discussion every four years. Inevitable, increasing frustration is the—forgive the expression— fall-out from the tension between an elitist technology and a perverse democratic vision.

To a significant degree, the frustrations of U.S. democracy, in the postwar years, were channelled into growth. If war could not serve as an outlet for democracy, then expansion could. Energy that once went into combat found itself diverted into increasing the GNP. When the energy gave out, the frustration doubled. If the major tasks of the modern state are to encourage growth and to prepare for war, what is one to do when growth has stopped and war is impossible? The rapid increase of Cold War sentiment since the middle of the Carter Administration can be directly traced to the sense of anger and disappointment in the United States caused by a democratic system that demands war and growth but cannot provide either.

Over the past two hundred years, as capital has become concentrated in ever more centralized forms, the means of violence have also become concentrated to a degree never before experienced. On the frontier, one always had one's rifle. In the nineteenth century, states played a considerable role in organizing the U.S. armed forces. Even in the twentieth century, World War II was fought with weapons that are laughable from the perspective of the 1980s. Yet between the start of World War II and its end, a remarkable change had come over the administration of war. "Out of this first war of both the mass and the machine," Walter Millis wrote, "this first truly global conflict, one salient and shocking fact was to emerge: the almost unbelievable power of the modern, centralized, managerial and nationalistic state to drain the whole physical, intellectual, economic, emotional and moral resources of its citizens to the single end of military victory."[97] Capitalists may extract surplus-value; the state extracts surplus security. Having given over to the state control over their destiny, people are unlikely to gamble with how the state uses that control. They have, after all, no other way to "protect" themselves.

With so much at stake, it is little wonder that rules of ordinary politics are suspended when insecurity becomes rife. As the U.S.-Iranian hostage crisis indicated, security, once it becomes an issue in an election debate, plunges quickly down to the lowest common denominator of discourse. Not having fought a war on its own turf for one hundred and twenty years, America is myopic on the subject to begin with. When combined with the state's monopolization of the means of security, hopes for rational debate and clear understanding on matters of war and peace evaporate. European societies can still, to some degree, conduct meaningful discussion of these issues within the confines of the electoral system; the U.S., apparently, cannot.

Perverse democracy has become an obstacle to peace. Political perversion has never been stronger than in the age of Reagan; the same goes for the threat of war. One of the prime tasks of the Wall Street, corporate liberal financial Establishment in the United States has been to keep people like Reagan from entering the White House. So long as U.S. foreign policy was made by an exclusive, undemocratic elite, it was always *somewhat*—there is Vietnam—under control. Now that the elite has been discredited, foreign policy is once again made through perverse democracy, and Reaganism is the result. Under a demagogic president, with fabulous ability to orchestrate fears and insecurity, perverse democracy has taken its place as a major contributor to the continuing arms race.

I am not arguing that perverse democracy "caused" the Cold War. Obviously one cannot dismiss the fact that a capitalist democracy and a socialist policy would engage in rivalry, whether either were perverted or not. Moreover, big-power rivalry has been a feature of world politics since the advent of the modern state and would exist independently of the internal organization of the participating states. Finally, war and its demands need not be linked to democracy; fascism proved to be as fully compatible, if not more so, with war-making requirements as perverse democracy. My point is simply that long historical trends which transformed democracy from a republican concern with virtue and propriety into an expanded, more participatory, but also more manipulable form, prepared the groundwork for participation in the Cold War. Raising questions about the Cold War necessarily raises questions about democracy as currently practiced. From a U.S. perspective, the Cold War continues because, at some level and no matter how distorted, the U.S. people have become convinced that they need it.

The Cold War has another side. If perverse democracy developed through war and consolidated through growth, the socialist state, again in practice if not in theory, developed to encourage growth and was solidified through war. In the East as well as the West, the perversion of one of the most humanistic and progressive traditions of the modern world bears substantial responsibility for the perpetuation of the Cold War.

Socialism Russian style, like democracy American style, originated in the trenches of World War I. It has been persuasively argued that the Russian Revolution took place at a time when international events unforeseen by the Bolsheviks (or by anyone else) so weakened the internal authority of the old regime that systemic transformation became possible.[98] World War I simultaneously destroyed the old socialist ideal of international solidarity and enhanced the new socialist ideal of the seizure of state power. If advanced capitalism was a product of the way the U.S. entered World War I, advanced socialism was an end result of the way Russia left it. Just as the war thoroughly changed the meaning of democracy, broadening it and narrowing it at the same time, the war changed the meaning of socialism, making it both more possible but also more problematic.

Unlike Americans, who, in the words of David Kennedy, "disproportionately used their profits from the war years to fuel a spectacular expansion of the home economy,"[99] the Russians came out of the war devastated and disunified. Socialism's first real challenge was whether it could grow, not whether it could fight. Who could imagine, reading the great nineteenth-century classics of socialist thought, that the main selling point of the idea in the twentieth century would be its ability to organize economic growth? Yet the crucial turning point for advanced socialism was the resolution of the debates in the 1920s over economic growth, symbolized by the defeat of Bukharin and the emergence of the Stalinist form of primitive accumulation. Bukharin's notions of balanced growth, attempting to reconcile the obvious need to expand with a recognition of the peasant character of Russia, was the last chance for Soviet socialism to avoid the perversions of modernity. Once the goal became industrial catch-up, socialism had as much chance to be faithful to its ideological origins as democracy did to its.

Stalinism was a strategy of economic growth, one, to be sure, filled with irrationality and terror beyond the human imagination, yet one also relentlessly single-minded in its pursuit of modernity. By transforming the countryside through liquidation, Stalin prepared the groundwork for the emergence of a modern proletariat. When World War II ended, two-thirds of the Soviet population lived off the land; in 1979, the figure was down to 38 percent. "The Russian muzhik," Daniel Singer writes, "is historically on his way out in the same way as the peasant has been vanishing in the western world."[100] Moreover, by promoting socialism in one country and sponsoring a nationalistic program, Stalin unified the nation state, weakening the autonomous republics and concentrating political and economic power in the hands of a centralized elite.[101] The net result was to enhance the Soviet state's capacity to carry out the two fundamental political tasks of modernity: industrial expansion and the ability to fight war.

By the 1940s, the Soviet state was, for the first time in Russian history, capable of meeting the West on its own terms. No consumer society had been created, but the level of heavy industrialization could not be denied. Both the industrial potential of the Soviet Union and its somewhat more urbanized and proletarianized working class contributed to the Soviet success in World War II. Especially when compared to the humiliation of the Japanese War of 1905 and the disastrous peace terms signed at Brest-Litovsk, the Russians had taken their socialist revolutions and, in the name of Stalin, transformed it into a state machinery capable of acting on twentieth century terms.

To ask whether Bukharinism would have been a "better" alternative to the Soviet Union is like asking whether Jeffersonianism is more appropriate to modern America than Hamiltonianism. Modernity does not allow such choices. Clearly, the pursuit of a Bukharinite strategy would have made the Soviets weaker in an age of war and growth. Without rapid and heavy industrialization, not only might the Russians have lost World War II but Hitlerian fascism could have been the future of postwar Europe. Stalin's accomplishment in Russia, like those of the state builders in the United States, was to revise a progressive and humanistic ideology to make it compatible with the tasks of the modern state. Socialism might not have survived without Stalin. It did survive, but it barely resembled socialism.

At some level, the Soviet Union is still "socialist," just as, at some level, the United States is still "democratic." In the Soviet Union the means of production are not in private hands, planning is the most prominent feature of economic life, there has been a marked tendency toward greater equality, and from time to time the Soviets act in support of socialist revolutions around the world. (Sometimes they do not, and in at least one case, the Ethiopian, they switched sides in the middle.) None of these advances, and advances they are, would have been possible without the consolidation of political power to expand economically and the consolidation of military power to ward off a threat to those gains. Yet the price paid for these accomplishments has been as great as the price paid in the United States to obtain women's suffrage, greater participation, and extensions of the welfare state—all products of the need to broaden the public realm in an age of perverse democracy. Perverse socialism is marked by top-down hierarchical decision-making, a controlled press and distrust of dissent, racial and ethnic chauvinism, industrial priorities, the militarization of society, and, most significant in the context of this chapter, a commitment to "keeping up" with the West that has, in its own fashion, contributed to the Cold War.

The Cold War has become intertwined with perverse socialism in the Soviet Union much as perverse democracy deforms the interventional behavior of the United States. Stalinism may have been a path, however monstrous, to primitive industrialization, but it was not in accord with the more bureaucratic and impersonal second phase of growth that followed World War II. As Seweryn Bialer has written about the Soviet elite: "They had been brought up in the midst of Stalin's barbarism; they were its willing participants; but now they yearned for a different, what they would consider a deserved and more stable, political lifestyle, for material progress, respectability, enjoyment." This in the deepest sense was the key reason why the system of mature Stalinism could not survive its creator. The leadership as a whole, and the elites, as a whole, wanted a new deal.[102] Growth rates flattened out after World War II, but they never stopped increasing: during the 1970s, a period of economic downturn, Soviet growth rates were still higher than American.[103] Having successfully launched Soviet society into the growth era, the Soviet state became responsible for the management of growth. Despite numerous economic problems, it has managed growth as well as can be expected for a society that so recently emerged into modernity.

In a similar fashion, Stalinism, appropriate for the kind of mass-mobilizing, labor-intensive war that World War II became, was highly counter-productive to the science-based, high technology, bureaucratic caution that emerged in the Cold War. Nuclear weapons played as much of a trick on Stalinism as they did on democracy. "World War II," Bialer writes, "can be seen as the turning point, when the almost miraculous victory upon the brink of total disaster made credible the attribution of nearly magical powers to Stalin, and his identification with this great patriotic achievement evoked widespread, genuine admiration."[104] The

Great Patriotic War, indeed, required massive sacrifice, positive participation, mobilization—all the very features of a political system that nuclear weapons deny. A cult of personality is intolerable when personalities can push buttons which would blow up the world. Trends toward the collectivization of war-making and military decisions, already well under way, were given an added impetus when science and technology were so devastatingly unleashed.

The Soviets, like the Americans, have a collective memory of war, but their recollections are different. War to the Russians means devastation so vast that it must, if possible, be avoided. To a significant degree the fact that the Soviets have generally taken the lead in arms control negotiations is a reflection of their more recent experience, at home, of the meaning of modern war. Yet fear of war, in a modernized state, does not lead to pacifism but its opposite. Precisely because the Russian people are horrified at the prospect of another devastation, they tacitly yield extraordinary power to their leaders to prevent it and their leaders use that power to build more weapons. The Soviet state is responsible both for making war and for insuring that it not be fought, a paradox that strengthens bureaucratic and impersonal tendencies in the military sector.

Socialism, then, was indispensible in transforming Russia from a feudal underdeveloped monarchy into a modern state capable of expanding and defending itself. It would be difficult to imagine, even if the course of history could, by some act of intellectual curiosity, be changed, that a moderate bourgeois regime emerging after World War I could have had such profound, and rapid, modernizing characteristics. Yet to achieve these extraordinary results, socialism has increasingly been divorced from its intellectual origins, perverted into a new doctrine that would make its contribution to the Cold War. The deformities of the Soviet system have been endlessly catalogued, more, I am sure, than the ills of any other social system in human history, so not much time need be spent on the subject. Nonetheless, it is worth reiterating the effect that such perversions as hierarchy, nationalism, and empire have had on the course of the first socialist revolution of the twentieth century.

Socialism, like democracy, has diverse, even contradictory, roots. Economic justice or more efficient planning—that was the question. Competition from the West answered it. "The dilemma of Soviet economic policy," Rudolf Bahro has written, "is reminiscent of the children's tale of the hare and the tortoise, where the tortoise bends the rules of the game. Each time the Soviet economy pauses for breath after a bout of exertion it hears a voice from the end of the course shout: "I'm already here."[105] Once the decision was taken to play catch-up with the west, hierarchy became inevitable. Growth, as the Reagan Administration has happily announced, requires a certain injustice; in the Soviet version of growth politics, a willingness to tolerate inequality became the price to be paid, not especially reluctantly, to expand the domestic economy. Military competition with the West reinforced that conclusion as strongly as economic competition initiated it, for war, and its preparation, requires hierarchy as fully as growth. A growth-oriented economy linked to a war machine is not likely to be a vehicle of social justice. Ironically, the Soviet leaders were not successful in matching the West economically. But they did achieve a certain equality in nuclear weapons, thereby legitimating the domestic inequities among the population.

War economies and growth economies have striking similarities. Studies of Third World regimes, for example, have demonstrated that military elites promote industrial values more consistently than they do values of equity, thereby accepting as given and unalterable international capitalist relationships.[106] In the Soviet case, perverse socialism became a mechanism for achieving growth and war planning simultaneously. At first, centralized economic planning possessed the sure advantage of channelling investment into war production without the cumbersome system of incentives and pay-offs characteristic of the West. The entire Soviet economy, as Oskar Lange once pointed out, began to look like a Western war economy, organized to achieve a specific objective.[107] Yet if socialism paved the way to fight war, over time the fighting of war began to serve as a model for the organization of socialism. Since World War II, and especially since the decision of the Soviet elite after the Cuban missile crisis to play serious military catch-up with the West, the defense sector establishes the goals and the economy is altered to meet them, not the other way around.[108] Socialism was once the end, and the strengthening of the state the means to reach it. Now enhancing the state is the goal, and socialism tailored to achieve that.

If liberalism is the ideology of the market, nationalism is the world-view of the state. Democracy in the West, originally hostile to liberalism, made its accommodations with it in the interests of growth. Socialism in the East, originally antithetical to nationalism, has transformed itself in its image for *raisons d'etat*. Growth and war are the concrete embodiments of the national spirit. Engaged in a grotesque competition to bring itself down to the level of the U.S.—though, in fairness, the U.S. under Reagan seems to determined to bring itself down to the level of the Soviet Union—the Russians have married the ideology of socialism to the interests of nationalism. The defense of socialism becomes the defense of the Soviet Union, and militarism and preparations for exterminism are clothed in the language of progressive humanism.

The ultimate deformity of socialism in the Soviet Union was reached with the Polish worker rebellions of 1980. Not only had socialism come to stand for hierarchy and national power, now it posed itself as a bulwark against—socialism. Americans who watched their government suppress democratic movements in Latin America in the name of democracy could only force wan smiles as they heard Soviet and Polish communists denounce a workers' revolution. In both cases the reason was the same: the protection of an empire rationalized by an originally anti-imperialist ideology. For the Russians to view events in Poland as an attack on socialism is to confuse an economic vision and the arms race imperatives of the Soviet state.

Socialism, once again in practice, not in theory, has emerged as a major contributor to the Cold War. Perverse socialism is as strongly embedded in the Kremlin as perverse democracy is in the White House. Moreover, there is every reason to expect an increase in perversion as events conspire against the Soviet elite. As state builders, the Kremlin leaders have come to depend, like all state builders, on growth and security. "If there is any single value that dominates the minds and thoughts of the Soviet establishment from the highest to the lowest level," Bialer writes, "it is the value of order; if there is any single fear that outweighs all the others, it is the fear of disorder, chaos, fragmentation, loss of control."[109] States bring order, and growth and war are the health of the state. Without them, disorder threatens. In the 1980s, threats of an economic crisis at home have combined with the limitations of empire abroad to frustrate and puzzle the Soviet leadership. America's response to disorder has been to choose a nostalgic Reaganism. Russia's occurs at a time when the entire Soviet elite faces a period of transition. Without a willingness to explore alternative sources of order, the two superpowers seem destined to strengthen the very features of their society that once gave them life, but now threaten them with extinction.

In the American literature on totalitarianism, recently revived with the published thoughts of Ambassador Kirkpatrick,[110] an unbreakable link is said to exist between the oppressive internal character of the Soviet Union and its expansionist external behavior. In the Soviet literature on imperialism, as Jerry Hough has

demonstrated, the exact mirror image is reflected: capitalist societies are said to expand because of their flawed internal organization.[111] Cold War scholarship conveniently blames, not only the
other side, but the other side's *system,* for the perpetuation of the
Cold War. With bad scholarship so bipartisanly consensual, one is
tempted to conclude that both are wrong and that internal structure has little to do with external behavior. But that oversimplifies.
Perverse democracy and perverse socialism are very much con-
nected to the behavior of the states that embody them, if in different, and important ways.

Contrary to the theory of totalitarianism, there is substantial
evidence that the *more* open a society, the greater its proclivity to
practice an aggressive foreign policy. As I have argued throughout
this book, America has been more susceptible to the most extreme
version of the Soviet threat, and therefore more inclined to be
belligerent, in exactly those periods when its politics were most
open to controversy. Each of the three periods of Cold War hostility
that I have described in this book took place on or near elections,
where different branches of government were supposed to be
checking each other, when the elite was disunified rather than
coordinated, and when the economy was in relatively good shape.
The inescapable conclusion presents itself: to the degree that
Ameican liberal democracy "works," to that degree America
becomes more suspicious, aggressive, and unilateral in its views of
foreign affairs. The one superpower that has the far more attractive internal politics has a far less attractive external politics.

Soviet expansionism has entirely different roots. Russia has
had a long history of imperial dreams, and the consolidation of state
power under a socialist regime has enabled those dreams to be
realized in a more systematic fashion than the periodic skirmishes
of the tsars. States with the power to expand will expand. It is
neither the economy of a society, nor its ideology, that compels
aggressive behavior in the international system. The state itself, as
the Weberian and Schumpeterian position holds, seeks the opportunity to consolidate its power, both at home and abroad. Economic
and ideological factors shape *how* that power is consolidated. The
importance of perverse socialism is that it affects the behavior of
the Soviet state in the Cold War, just as perverse democracy affects
the behavior of the United States. The asymmetry in the Cold War
is due to the fact that the behavior induced by each perversion is
distinct.

As a highly centralized, authoritarian state, the Soviet Union
practices a quite different kind of imperial politics from that of the

United States. The absence of competing political parties, combined with the lack of freedom of thought and expression, ironically removes one of the pressures toward inconsistent imperial behavior. Whereas the United States *politicizes* its path toward empire, the Soviet Union approaches its hegemony *managerially*. The Russians are far more interested in fashioning agreed-upon rules for imperial conduct than the United States. Dictatorships seem so much more compatible with the smooth management of empire than democracies—surely a major reason why imperialists in the United States continuously seek restrictions on a free press and on popular inquiry. Soviet leaders need not fear that the agreements they make in the international system will be distorted and ridiculed in the emotions of an election campaign. Nor need they worry that secrets will be "leaked" in a fashion requiring them to disown them. There is less of a gap in the Soviet Union between the demands of empire abroad and the management of empire at home.

This is not to suggest an absence of pluralistic pressures. There are interest groups in Soviet politics, and splits within the elite over relations with the United States are very real. Moreover the Soviet Union at the moment is in the throes of a generational transition more significant than any in its history. In 1980 the average age of the full members of the Politburo was 70.1, compared to 61.0 in 1964 and 55.4 in 1952. Andrei Gromyko first came to Washington when Roosevelt was president. Boris Ponomarev, Central Committee Secretary, was named to the executive committee of the Comintern when Jimmy Carter was twelve and Edward Kennedy four.[113] (Ronald Reagan, however, was a ripe twenty-five). The Russians not only have the oldest elite in the world, it is one that has served together longest because the Stalinist purges removed an entire generation from office. Such a massive transition in leadership as the Russians will soon experience may make the smooth management of empire more difficult, perhaps leading to the kinds of unpredictable actions that characterize the United States.

Nonetheless, just as perverse democracy shapes the character of America's foreign affairs, perverse socialism acts to color the Russian approach. The Russians approach their empire the way an *oblast* manager approaches his region. Planning, only moderately successful at home, is inevitably extended abroad. Kremlinology is more of an exact science than Americanology. They always seem puzzled at what we do; we are rarely puzzled at what they do. Sometimes the Russians find in Washington a planner like Kissinger who shares their urgency about imperial management. Just when they think they have cut a deal, a new administration comes to power—there have been five American presidents between 1968 and 1981—determined to repudiate his predecessor's policies. A Reagan or a Weinberger, when he denounces the Russians, objects to the existence of a Soviet empire. Soviet abusive rhetoric denounces the fact that the Americans have an empire less than their refusal to share it.

From the standpoint of preventing nuclear war, managerialism is preferable to politicization. The uncertainty and immaturity coming from Washington continuously upsets whatever momentum toward arms control is established, while the Russians, who are second to move in their pursuit of self-interest, are more likely to see that self-interest is realized through big-power agreements. When perverse politics interconnect with the Cold War, a drastic irony results. That party to the Cold War which has a far preferable domestic system has the more dangerous foreign policy, while the party that has a horrendous internal organization acts with greater external restraint at a time when primitive impulses are impossible to contemplate. The very lack of anything resembling democracy in the Soviet Union places restraints on its behavior abroad. The very presence of democracy in the United States, especially of the perverse type, undermines its ability to act as a mature power. Skeptics might ask themselves whether at the height of the Iranian-American hostage crisis, they would have been willing to put the question of the use of tactical nuclear weapons in Iran on the ballot, at a time when "Nuke the Ayatollah" bumper stickers were proliferating.

Yet while managerial predictability is certainly preferable to political instability, to have to choose between the two would be like the kind of option a condemned prisoner might make between the hangman's noose and the gas chamber. Soviet nuclear weapons are as dangerous to the world, by their very existence, as American nuclear weapons. One side may indicate more willingness to establish rules for the arms race, but neither is serious about bringing it to an end. Relief from the madness of the arms race will have to come from somewhere beyond both perverse democracy *and* perverse socialism. The U.S. and the Soviet Union are too locked into their mutual *danse macabre* to offer the peace movement much hope.

Yet there is, nonetheless, hope for peace. Within the peripheries of perverse democracy and perverse socialism there has been discovered, of all things, democracy and socialism. Demonstrators in Western Europe have been campaigning against nuclear weapons and, in the process, reminding the world that democracy is possible in a democracy. Workers in Poland have been campaigning against Soviet perversions and, in the process, informing us that socialism is possible under socialism. What ultimately gives perverse democracy and perverse socialism their mobilizing power is also what makes democracy and socialism too important to be left to those who speak in their name. So long as human beings value life, the original radical impulses in both doctrines will constantly come to the surface, in the process saving not only the doctrines, but perhaps the world as well.

CHAPTER IX

MEETING THE THREAT
FROM THE SOVIET THREAT

If a perverse form of democracy has produced an exaggerated fear of the threat from abroad, only a return to a more popularly-based democracy can bring about balance and perspective in American foreign policy. The Cold War has as much to do with the way Americans struggle with each other as it does with the way America struggles with the Soviet Union. In the early 1980s Americans are debating foreign policy with an intensity not seen in a generation. From town meetings and the grassroots, organized in a genuinely Jeffersonian fashion, there has arisen a movement for a nuclear freeze that has had an astonishing and unexpected impact on American politics. From Washington and on television, in accord with neo-Hamiltonian realities, there is an administration trying to sell the American people security through weapons, many of them enormously destabilizing. How this struggle between two different versions of democracy is resolved involves nothing less than, as one writer has put it, the fate of the earth.[114] No issue can have more significant impact on the future than the question of how America resolves its feelings about the Soviet threat now.

Throughout this book I have argued that the Cold War hysteria which increased in the Reagan Administration, despite obvious differences, has some important similarities with the two previous peaks in anti-Soviet perceptions. This latest version of the Cold War began under a Democrat attempting to head off the right only to find himself victimized by it. It occurred at a time when relations between President and Congress were suspicious and awkward, working their way into policy considerations where they did not belong. Interservice rivalries at the start of the 1980s were as strong as ever, given the greater cost of new weapons systems combined with less ability to pay for them. Foreign policy elites, in disarray since Vietnam, were not above using the Soviet threat to reorient America toward a global reassertion of imperial ambitions. And finally a serious economic downturn brought to power an administration committed to growth, expansion, and militarism as a resolution to the American crisis, even though growth, expansion, and militarism caused the crisis in the first place. Ronald Reagan is a conservative Republican, while Harry Truman and John F. Kennedy fancied themselves liberal Democrats; that obvious and important difference aside, Reagan's Cold War is not dissimilar from its predecessors'. All of them have important domestic roots.

If I am correct that there is a significant domestic basis to the rise and fall of the Soviet threat, then the whole question of Russia's intentions becomes a political question, answered not only by what they do, but also by how we interpret what they do. And our interpretations are inevitably influenced by the political configurations that exist in this country. When America feels secure about itself and is confident of its goals, it worries less about the Soviet threat and goes about its business. When America feels uncertain, insecure, gripped by crisis, its loses track of its own mission and focuses its anxiety on the external enemy. The more secure we are at home, in short, the less our need to project insecurity abroad, but the more insecure our domestic politics, the greater our concern with external security. One of the genuine weaknesses of the Reagan agenda, and one reason why the American people are growing tired of it, is that in order to convince Americans of an external threat, it must emphasize negative aspects of the United States like its alleged military inferiority. Not all Americans are prepared to accept that they are as weak and helpless as Mr. Reagan says they are.

The present political conjuncture in the United States could either move it along toward a positive and secure attempt to work out its problems or continue its unhealthy, stereotyped, and negative quest to blame its problems on everyone else. It is as clear a choice as a people are ever given: solve your own problems and you will not need to fear an alien enemy; delude yourself into thinking that all your problems lie with the other guy and you will seek a spurious security that will just make you feel more vulnerable.

For all these reasons, I believe that the best way to meet the Soviet threat, or any external threat to America's security, is by creating a democratic and progressive social movement that will address questions of domestic security. America needs a balast to the influence of the right, a movement from below capable of demanding the kind of security and sense of self that grows out of sharing real control over one's life. There is indeed a threat to the United States, but it comes not from the Soviet Union but from a tendency to blame others for uncertainty instead of working together to build democracy and community. America—in fact the whole world—faces a clear and present danger from the Soviet threat. It is, however, not the threat from Russia that runs the risk of destroying democracy in the United States but the threat posed by those who would acquire extremely destabilizing weapons systems for reasons that have little to do with national security and much to do with politics. There are any number of powerful policymakers and institutions that would, in the name of preserving freedom, centralize political power in undemocratic ways; curtail civil liberties in order to protect them; create a highly monopolistic economy that would be inflationary and inefficient; suspend or cut back social welfare programs if they interfere with the defense budget; militarize American values; intervene throughout the world whenever they felt it justified; support the most racist regimes in order to protect us from communism; force the United States to resemble the authoritarian countries against which it is allegedly struggling; and develop dangerous new nuclear weapons that would destabilize the existing balance. It is vital, in my view, for the United States to find a way to protect itself against this threat.

Because there is such a substantial political core to the waxing and waning of the Soviet threat, the danger that America faces from within can only be met *politically*. The threat from those who try to exaggerate the Soviet threat will be met only when a political challenge has been issued to the dominant way that public business is conducted in the United States.

As I have tried to point out in this essay, the Soviet threat has become a regular feature of American life because it is essential to each of the following processes:

1. It enables the Democratic Party—but now the Republican Party as well—to govern without developing a program for reorganizing social life along positive lines, while protecting itself from the demagoguery of the right;

2. It is a useful device to prop up the necessity of a strong executive in the face of popular feeling that political power should be broken up and kept weak;

3. It has enabled bureaucratic vested interests—particularly in the military services—to retain their hold over the federal budget while other interests seek inroads into what they have;

4. It has been the method by which foreign policy coalitions with unpopular ideas (free trade, extensive foreign aid, the recreation of empire) have mobilized public and interest group support for a shift in the locus of American foreign policy;

5. Finally, it has permitted advocates of greater economic growth to develop a method of stimulating the economy through federal spending without supporting controversial programs that would arouse opposition from business and conservative groups.

The way to meet the threat from the Soviet threat is to create a progressive political presence in the United States, one that can rectify the rightward tilt that exists on all foreign policy and defense issues. Contained in this unremarkable assertion are two imperatives. First, those who are attempting to build a progressive coalition in America—including local activists, community organizers, church groups, labor unions, and minorities—must take foreign policy issues more seriously than they have. Without some curtailment of cold war rhetoric, there simply will not be any advances in affirmative action, community control over economic development, labor union organizing, or any other such issue. And secondly it means that the peace groups and anti-militarist organizations which have been concerned with foreign policy need to combine a preoccupation with moral witness and individual conscience with a larger political understanding of the world that illustrates why militarism has become such a crucial aspect of American politics. When both of these changes occur, a solid basis for an anti-militarist coalition will be laid.

Such a coalition has at the present time a major opportunity to develop a program that would have overwhelming popular support in the United States. Unlike all previous peaks of the Soviet threat, the third upturn that began after 1978 comes at a time when the economy is in a state of fairly permanent stagnation. This means that the United States simply cannot afford what its alleged protectors will demand. Moreover, if belt-tightening is achieved in order to increase U.S. rearmament, the long-term economic consequences would be extraordinarily severe. Whatever "security" the

American people would feel by having Trident submarines and MX missiles would in no time be undermined by the inflation, poor economic performance, and balance-of-payment problems that would directly follow from building them. There is a big difference between spending money on arms when it seems to stimulate economic growth and spending money on arms when there is very little money around. The cold warriors are more economically vulnerable in the early 1980s than they have ever been.

But economic vulnerablity will not be turned into an asset for those who want to see a secure and stable future for the United States unless they are able to expand their program into one that has mass appeal. The nuclear freeze campaign offers an opportunity to do just that. In part because of the economic costs of the new Cold War, but also because Ronald Reagan's war-fighting plans simply cannot withstand public scrutiny, peace groups have taken the initiative for the first time since the 1960s. There is only one side in any public discussion of nuclear war, and that is the peace side. In an unbelievably inept way, Ronald Reagan has made nuclear war a public issue where he cannot help losing. So long as people do not think about nuclear war, military men tend to get whatever they want. But when people do begin to think, or are forced to by remarkably irresponsible rhetoric from the White House, they have no trouble deciding who is responsible for their sense of insecurity and worry.

A massive peace campaign could take heart from the kinds of issues addressed in this report. I have tried to show how, time after time, elites that possessed relatively unpopular ideas—such as a strong executive, an expensive public sector, an inflationary program, an emphasis on large-scale production, and a demand for domestic sacrifice to stabilize the world economy—have managed to stifle the strong opposition to their vision by manipulating the Soviet threat. The task, then, is to try to take off the husk of the Soviet threat, which does have mass appeal, so that the kernel of an undemocratic and monopolistic economic program, which does not, will be revealed.

To raise the issue of the Soviet threat, therefore, is to raise questions about the whole direction that the American political system has taken since the New Deal. It is to ask questions like these:

1. Do we need a presidency so strong that all other political institutions in America, including political parties, legislative bodies, and dissenting traditions wither?

2. What have been the costs of relying on a governing coalition that has sought to secure such a firm place in the center of the political spectrum that it has stifled public debate, contributed to an apolitical cynicism, and enabled policymakers to satisfy their self interest without public scrutiny?

3. If a free-trade world order demands that we accept unemployment due to the export of jobs, declining productivity and innovation at home, and the use of the dollar to facilitate world trade, have the costs of relying on worldwide economic growth become too expensive for the American people?

4. Do we need to rely on an economy that organizes itself from the top down, restricts competition, and finances its growth through inflationary and inefficient boondoggles like the military budget?

5. Can we afford to allow the protectors of our security, especially the military services and all the constituents that surround them, to protect themselves against each other by passing the costs on to everyone else?

The answers to these questions are not obvious. There are times and situations where strong leadership may be necessary. One should not necessarily cut oneself off from the world economy. Sometimes inflation has to be accepted in order to achieve other goals. Competitive capitalism is not in itself a good thing, especially if it exploits labor, as it tends to do. But these are issues that the American people need to discuss, and so long as the Soviet threat dominates the political agenda, they are issues that probably will not be discussed.

As the 1980s progress, America seems uncertain of itself. Its political future is clouded. There is an air of unpredictability about its role in the world. Its discourse has turned ugly. There is a general feeling throughout the land that something has gone wrong, that the dream has been spoiled. Prophets of doom and withdrawal abound. At the same time, all of those forces that stand for decency, fairness, and peace have begun to arouse themselves from a prolonged stupor. There is a sense of movement and change, a feeling that the current impasse is as much an opportunity as a possible debacle. As America chooses between a narrow and nasty retreat into selfishness and an opportunity to restructure itself so as to face the future with its humanity and tolerance intact, few questions will be more important than that of the Soviet threat. If

Americans wake up to the danger posed from those within their midst who would destroy the best features of their country in order to militarize it against a misunderstood enemy, they have a chance to create the kind of future that they will then deserve.

FOOTNOTES

1. *New York Times*, March 9, 1981, cited in Fred Halliday, *The Making of the Second Cold War* (London: Verso, 1983). Despite differences in emphasis and interpretation, I am indebted to Halliday's excellent coverage of the rise of Cold War hostility under Carter and Reagan.
2. Ronald Brownstein and Nina Easton, *Reagan's Ruling Class* (New York: Pantheon, 1982). See also Jerry Sanders, *Peddlers of Crisis* (Boston: South End Press, 1983).
3. "United States Defense Policy," News Release, Office of Assistant Secretary of Defense, *Public Affairs*, April 20, 1982, p. 2.
4. *New York Times,* May 22, 1982, p. 1.
5. *New York Times,* June 4, 1982, p. 1.
6. *New York Times,* June 1, 1982, p. 23.
7. Committee on the Present Danger, *What is the Soviet Union Up To?*, p. 10; Lt. Gen. Daniel Graham in *United States/Soviet Strategic Options,* Hearings before the Senate Foreign Relations Subcommittee on Arms Control, Oceans and International Environment, 95th Congress, First Session (1977), p. 123. Both cited in Les Aspin, "What are the Russians Up To?" *International Security* (Summer 1978), p. 30.
8. Keynote Speech, Eighth Annual National Security Conference, National Defense University, July 13-15, "U.S. Military Strategy for the 1980s," pp. 2-3.
9. Aspin, p. 42.
10. Andrew Cockburn, *The Threat* (New York: Random House, 1983).

11. Aspin, p. 49.

12. Mary Kaldor, *The Baroque Arsenal* (New York: Hill and Wang, 1981) and James Fallows, *National Defense* (New York: Random House, 1981).

13. For a recent illustration of this thesis, see Robert A. Dalleck, *The American Style of Foreign Policy* (New York: Knopf, 1983).

14. See Joseph Finder, *Red Carpet* (New York: New Republic Books, 1983) to see how one writer finds that his distaste for the Soviet Union is much greater than his love for capitalism.

15. Daniel Yergin, *Shattered Peace* (Boston: Houghton Mifflin Co., 1978), pp. 17-68.

16. *Ibid.,* p. 82

17. *Ibid.,* p. 83.

18. An interesting treatment of these men is contained in Martin Weil, *A Pretty Good Club* (New York: W. W. Norton & Co., 1978), pp. 385-442.

19. NSC-68, which was declassified in 1975, is reprinted in Thomas H. Etzold and John Lewis Gaddis (eds.), *Containment: Documents on American Policy and Strategy, 1945-1950* (New York: Columbia University Press, 1978), pp. 385-442.

20. Dean Acheson, *Present at the Creation* (New York: W. W. Norton & Co., 1969), p. 374.

21. John Lewis Gaddis, *Russia, the Soviet Union, and the United States* (New York: John Wiley and Sons, 1978), p. 207.

22. *Ibid.,* p. 209.

23. Walter Lafeber, *America, Russia, and the Cold War, 1945-66* (New York: John Wiley and Sons, 1967), pp. 209-210.

24. Samuel P. Huntington, *The Common Defense* (New York: Columbia University Press, 1961), p. 87. Huntington points out the difference between NSC-68 and the New Look: the former was a national *security* policy, the latter only a national policy. For this reason, the Eisenhower Administration rarely exaggerated Soviet military strength, as later administrations were to do: "Administration leaders frequently deprecated Soviet capabilities, particularly in airpower..." p. 69.

25. *Ibid.,* p. 95.

26. These figures are calculated from Barry M. Blechman and Stephen S. Kaplan, *Force Without War: U.S. Armed Forces as a Political Instrument* (Washington: Brookings Institution, 1978), pp. 547-553.

27. *Deterrence and Survival in the Nuclear Age* (The "Gaither Report "Gaither Report of 1957"), prepared for the use of the Joint Committee on Defense Production, Congress of the United States (Washington: U.S. Government Printing Office, 1976).

28. Maxwell Taylor, *The Uncertain Trumpet* (New York: Harper and Harper and Printand Harper and Row, 1960).

29. Henry Kissinger, *Nuclear Weapons and Foreign Policy* (New York: Harper and Row, 1957).

30. For critical assessments of Kennedy's foreign policy adventurism, see Richard J. Walton, *Cold War and Counterrevolution: The Foreign Policy of JFK* (New York: Viking Press, 1972) and Louise FitzSimmons, *The Kennedy Doctrine* (New York: Random House, 1972).

31. Kennedy's penchant for crises is dissected in Henry Fairlie, *The Kennedy Promise: The Politics of Expectation* (Garden City: Doubleday & Co., 1973).

32. Lafeber, p. 202.

33. William Shawcross, *Sideshow: Kissinger, Nixon and the Destruction of Cambodia* (New York: Simon and Schuster, 1979). See also Seymour Hersch, *The Price of Power* (New York: Summit Books, 1983).

34. For details of how Nixon won approval for SALT I from the Pentagon and Senate, see John Newhouse, *Cold Dawn* (New York: Holt, Rinehart and Winston, 1973).

35. Henry A. Kissinger, *American Foreign Policy* (New York: W. W. Norton & Co., 1974), pp. 89, 59.

36. Calculated from *Economic Report of the President,* transmitted to the Congress, January, 1978 (Washington: U.S. Government Printing Office, 1978), p. 257.

37. Blechman and Kaplan, *op cit.*

38. Cited in Wolfe and Sanders, *op cit.*

39. Richard Pipes, "Why the Soviet Union Thinks It Could Fight a Nuclear War and Win," *Commentary* 64 (July 1977), pp. 21-34.

40. Interview with Wolfe and Sanders. Cited in *op cit.*

41. On Team B, see also John Prados, *The Soviet Estimate* (New York: Dial, 1982), pp. 248-257.

42. Marshall D. Shulman, "Overview of U.S.-Soviet Relations," The Department of State, *Statement,* October 26, 1977.

43. For a more detailed examination, see Alan Wolfe, *America's Impasse* (Boston: South End Press, 1982).

44. Barton J. Berstein, "Economic Policies," in Richard S. Kirkendall (ed.), *The Truman Period as a Research Field* (Columbia, MO.: University of Missouri Press, 1967).

45. For an account of anti-communist liberalism see Mary Sperling McAuliffe, *Crisis on the Left: Cold War Politics and American Liberals, 1947-54* (Amherst, Mass.: University of Massachusetts Press, 1978).

46. See Samuel P. Huntington, *Political Order in Changing Society* (New Haven: Yale University Press, 1968), pp. 98-138.

47. On the increasing role of the state in the twentieth century, see Gabriel Kolko, *Main Currents in American History* (New York: Harper and Row 1976).

48. Bert Cochran, *Harry Truman and the Crisis Presidency* (New York: Funk and Wagnalls, 1973).

49. Yergin, pp. 282-83.

50. *Ibid.,* p. 351.

51. Arthur M. Schlesinger, Jr., *A Thousand Days* (Greenwich, Conn.: Fawcett Books, 1965), p. 117.

52. Richard P. Nathan, *The Plot that Failed: Nixon and the Administrative Presidency* (New York: John Wiley and Sons, 1975).

53. Joseph A. Califano, Jr., *A Presidential Nation* (New York: W. W. Norton & Co., 1975), p. 11.

54. Blechman and Kaplan, pp. 119-123.

55. On the background to these debates see Demetrios Caraley, *The Politics of Military Unification* (New York: John Wiley and Sons, 1975).

56. Morris Janowitz, *Social Control of the Welfare State* (New York: Elsevier North-Holland, 1976), p. 37.

57. President's Air Policy Commission, *Survival in the Air Age* (Washington: U.S. Government Printing Office, 1948).

58. Cited in Yergin, p. 341.

59. Franz Schurman, *The Logic of World Power* (New York: Pantheon Books, 1974), p. 154.

60. Taylor, *op. cit.*

61. Quoted in *New York Times,* April 8, 1982, p. B8.

62. *Ibid.*

63. Quoted in *Ibid.*

64. Quoted in *New York Times*, April 11, 1982, p. 24.

65. On the Asia-first outlook see Thomas McCormick, *China Market: America's Quest for Informal Empire* (Chicago: Quadrangle, 1967). The distinction between Asia-firsters and Europhiles is similar to Schurman's distinction between expansionists and imperialists. See Schurman, pp. 4-30.

66. On the Europeanist inclinations behind the Marshall Plan see Fred L. Block, *The Origins of International Economic Disorder* (Berkeley and Los Angeles: University of California Press, 1977), pp. 70-108.

67. For details on this period, see Richard M. Freeland, *The Truman Doctrine and the Origins of McCarthyism* (New York: Schocken Books, 1974).

68. Block, pp. 114-137.
69. Jim F. Heath, *Decade of Disillusionment: The Kennedy-Johnson Years* (Bloomington: Indiana University Press, 1975). Heath notes why Kennedy decided to make a stand over Berlin: "Being tough in foreign affairs was an effective technique for shutting off right-wing criticism, and, politically, he could afford to do so because the disorganized left and the independent liberals had no alternative but to support his administration." (p. 89).
70. I recall, as a teenager, how the Berlin Wall became a symbol of all the evils of communism. Yet in retrospect, a wall is more a symbol of the bankruptcy of the Soviet system, not its expansion. What could be more self-revealing than this attempt to shut off experience from a presumed social revolution?
71. Schlesinger, *A Thousand Days,* p. 541.
72. This point has been made by a number of marxist critics, especially Samir Amin, *Accumulation on a World Scale* (New York: Monthly Review Press, 1974).
73. W. W. Rostow, *The Stages of Economic Growth,* Second Edition, (Cambridge: Cambridge University Press, 1971,), p. 164.
74. Kissinger, p. 105.
75. Leslie Gelb and Richard Bates, *The Irony of Vietnam: The System Worked* (Washigton: Brookings Institution, 1979).
76. There were, however, ambiguities in the notion of containment since its inception. For a thorough history see John Lewis Gaddis, *Strategies of Containment* (New York: Oxford University Press, 1982).
77. Paul Baran and Paul Sweezy, *Monopoly Capitalism* (New York: Monthly Review Press, 1967).
78. Seymour Melman, *The Permanent War Economy* (New York: Simon and Schuster, 1974).
79. James O'Connor, "The Meaning of Economic Imperialism," in Robert I. Rhodes (ed.), *Imperialism and Underdevelopment: A Reader* (New York: Monthly Review Press, 1970), pp. 101-150. See S. M. Miller *et. al,* "Does the U.S. Economy Require Imperialism?" *Social Policy* 1 (September-October 1970), pp. 12-19 for a critique of this point of view.
80. Etzkold and Gaddis, *op. cit.*
81. Arthur Schlesinger, Jr. *Robert Kennedy and His Times* (Boston: Houghton Mifflin Co., 1978), p. 407.
82. Harold D. Lasswell, *National Security and Individual Freedom* (New York: 1950), pp. 23-49.
83. Randolph Bourne, *The Radical Will: Selected Writings, 1911-1918,* (New York 1977.)

144   Footnotes

84. Quoted in Paul Fussell, *The Great War and Modern Memory,* (New York: Oxford University Press, 1975), p. 13.
85. See Robert D. Cuff, *The War Industries Board* (Baltimore: Johns Hopkins University Press, 1973).
86. Quoted in Fussell, p. 320.
87. Alan Wolfe, "Presidential Power and the Crisis of Modernization," *Democracy,* Vol. 1, Number 2, April 1981, pp. 10-32.
88. Walter Karp, *The Politics of War* (New York: Harper & Row, 1979).
89. Cited in Raymond Aron, *The Century of Total War* (Boston: Beacon Press, 1954), p. 89.
90. Quoted in David Kennedy, *Over Here: The First War and American Society* (New York: Oxford University Press, 1980), p. 17.
91. Marc Ferro, *The Great War, 1914-1918,* (London: Routledge and Kegan Paul, 1973) p. 8.
92. William E. Leuchtenberg, "The New Deal and the Analogue of War" in John Braeman *et. al, Change and Continuity in Twentieth century America* (Columbus, Ohio: Ohio State University Press, 1964), pp. 105, 125.
93. "Yet today America can learn more from West Point than West Point from America. Upon the soldiers, the defenders of order, rests a heavy reponsibility. The greatest service they can render is to remain true to themselves, to serve with silence and courage in the military way. If they abjure the military spirit, they destroy themselves first and their nation ultimately. If the civilians permit the soldiers to adhere to the military standard, the nations themselves may eventually find redemption and security in making that standard their own." Samuel P. Huntington, *The Soldier and the State* (New York: Vintage, 1964), p. 466.
94. This paragraph is based on the material in Gregg Herken, *The Winning Weapon: The Atomic Bomb in the Cold War, 1945-1950* (New York: Knopf, 1981), pp. 30-31.
95. Raymond Williams, "The Politics of Nuclear Disarmament," *New Left Review* 124, November-December 1980.
96. A persuasive case that nuclear weapons have acted as a deterrent is made by Michael Mandelbaum, *The Nuclear Question: The United States and Nuclear Weapons, 1964-1976* (Cambridge: Harvard University Press, 1979).
97. Walter Millis, *Arms and Men* (New York: Mentor Books, 1956), p. 265.
98. Theda Skocpol, *States and Social Revolutions* (Cambridge: Cambridge University Press, 1979).

99. Kennedy, p. 346.

100. Daniel Singer, *The Road to Gdansk* (New York: Monthly Review Press, 1981), p. 93.

101. See Alvin Gouldner, "Stalinism: A Study of Internal Colonialism," *Telos* 34, Winter 1978.

102. Seweryn Bialer, *Stalin's Successors* (Cambridge: Cambridge University Press, 1980), p. 46.

103. Jerry Hough, *Soviet Leadership in Transition* (Washington: Brookings Institution, 1980), p. 131. Bialer agrees, "The major conclusion that emerges from our presentation of Soviet performance in the Brezhnev era is that the Soviet regime has by and large been able to deliver the goods; it has generally been able to satisfy popular expectations for higher standards of living." Bialer, *op. cit.,* p. 154.

104. Bialer, *op. cit.,* p. 30.

105. Rudolf Bahro, *The Alternative in Eastern Europe* (London: New Left Books, 1978), p. 134.

106. See, for example, R. N. Tannanhill, "The Performance of Military and Civilian Governmer ˙n South America, 1948-67," *Journal of Political and Military S   logy,* Vol. 4, No. 2, Fall 1976); Eric A. Nordlinger, "Soldiers in Mufti: The Impact of Military Rule upon Economic and Social Change in the Non-Western States," *American Political Science Review,* Vol. LXIV, No. 4, December, 1970 and the similar literature cited in Mary Kaldor, *The Baroque Arsenal* (New York: Hill and Wang, 1981), pp. 157-162.

107. Oskar Lange, *Essays in Capitalism and Socialism* (Oxford: Oxford University Press, 1970), cited in Kaldor, *op. cit.* p. 113.

108. Kaldor, *op cit.* pp. 99-129.

109. Bialer, *op cit.* pp. 145.

110. Jeane Kirkpatrick, "Dictatorships and Double Standards," *Commentary,* November 1975, and "U.S. Security and Latin America," *Commentary,* January 1981.

111. Jerry Hough, *The Soviet Union and Social Science Theory* (Cambridge: Harvard University Press, 1977).

112. For considerably more detail on this point, see Alan Wolfe, *America's Impasse, op. cit.*

113. Hough, *Soviet Leadership in Transition.*

114. Jonathan Schell, *The Fate of the Earth* (New York: Knopf, 1982).